Esquire

Drink Like a Man

Esquire

DRINK

Like a

Man

The
Only
Cocktail
Guide
Anyone
Really
Needs

Introduction by
DAVID GRANGER
Edited by
ROSS McCAMMON and
DAVID WONDRICH

CHRONICLE BOOKS
SAN FRANCISCO

A whole lot of thanks go to . . .

Jessie Kissinger, formerly of *Esquire*, whose work involved every page of this book; and who compiled, tested, and edited the recipes in "A Little Something to Eat, Maybe?"

All of the chefs who contributed those recipes.

Esquire's research director Bob Scheffler and the research staff of *Esquire*, who fact-checked much of the work in this book and who never get enough credit for what they do.

And Ryan D'Agostino, formerly of *Esquire*, and Lorena Jones, formerly of Chronicle Books, who decided this is a book that should exist, likely over drinks.

Library of Congress Cataloging-in-Publication Data:
Names: Chronicle Books (Firm)
Title: Drink like a man : the only cocktail guide anyone really needs.
Description: San Francisco : Chronicle Books, [2016] | Includes index.
Identifiers: LCCN 2015032398 | ISBN 9781452132709 (hardcover)
Subjects: LCSH: Cocktails. | LCGFT: Cookbooks.
Classification: LCC TX951 .E87 2016 | DDC 641.87/4—dc23
LC record available at http://lccn.loc.gov/2015032398

Manufactured in China

Designed by Erin Jang
Image on page 37 is credited to Nigel Cox.

Chronicle books and gifts are available at special quantity discounts to corporations, professional associations, literacy programs, and other organizations. For details and discount information, please contact our premiums department at corporatesales@chroniclebooks.com or at 1-800-759-0190.

10 9 8 7 6 5 4 3 2 1

Chronicle Books LLC
680 Second Street
San Francisco, California 94107
www.chroniclebooks.com

CONTENTS

How to Drink

The Drinks (and a little food)

The Classics

14 Drinks Every Man Should Know How to Make

Introduction

At *Esquire*, we drink. We don't drink thoughtlessly. We don't generally drink aggressively. But we drink. It's part of our lives, both work and social and, to us, it seems as if drinking improves both parts. We think a lot about drinking and, as a result, have theories about drinking, and strong opinions (don't get me started on "the measured pour" of neat liquor). We feel as though we've earned the opinions expressed in this book, both through experience and by virtue of the graduate course in drinking Dave Wondrich has been teaching us for the past fifteen years or so. Nobody knows more about the mechanics and rituals and particulars of drinking than Mr. Wondrich. He has literally written the book on cocktails (*Imbibe!*) and taught most of the great bartenders in America their craft. Dave is supremely knowledgeable without ever being didactic, and we hope that we can say the same about ourselves. With the exception of the recipes and some of the techniques presented here, most of the advice in this book is offered as suggestions toward better living through drinking. Accept or reject them, but know that they have worked for us.

I should note here that this manual does not aspire to be a comprehensive encyclopedia of drinks. There are *lots* of drinks in here. But there are thousands of drinks that have been made and served that you will not find here. What we offer is a collection of cocktails that are (a) fundamental, (b) important, (c) delicious or otherwise interesting, and (d) not full of shit. I understand this. For about ten months in the great American city of Chicago, I tended bar to make a living. What we chose *not* to serve was as important as what we served. We had just about everything a human could reasonably expect but, for instance, we did not have a blender. We did not have tap beer (this was long before the craft beer revolution and better beers were available only in bottles). We did not serve Malibu rum. It wasn't that kind of a place. Neither is this book.

With *Esquire*'s *Drink Like a Man*, we hope to improve your drinking life. And we take encouragement from the realization that a man with a drink in his hand is never alone.

—David Granger
editor in chief, *Esquire*

How to Drink

HOW

to use

This Book

~~~~~~

BY DAVID WONDRICH

Drink Like a Man. First off, I should say that by "man" here we mean anyone, regardless of gender, who's okay drinking a dry gin martini with a skewer of olives in it; who will sip a little whiskey neat from time to time; who appreciates a good IPA but will slug down the occasional High Life if that's what there is to drink; who thinks wine goes with food just fine; who doesn't consider a pink cocktail or a thin-stemmed glass some sort of test of gender identity (or, for that matter, gender solidarity). Anyone who drinks like an adult.

As much as we love beer and wine, though, this book is, for the most part, about cocktails (and sours, punches, fizzes, slings, nogs . . .). That's because learning to mix such things well takes rather more work than learning to open a bottle and pour it into a glass, and we firmly believe

that such work is worth performing. Why? We could say it's because it will help you resist the hype that lies behind so many trendy cocktails, or because it's a craft, and mastering any craft will make you a better, more self-sufficient person. But really, it's enough to say that mixing excellent drinks is fun and easy—but not *too* easy—and your friends will like you for it. And, when you're sitting down to the perfect Sazerac you've just stirred up at the end of a long day of dealing with whatever your job flings at you, so will you.

We've tried to give you the basics—the tools you'll need and how to use them and a few essential mixers that you'll need to keep around. We haven't wasted a lot of space on pocket guides to all the spirits you'll need; in our experience, for those to be detailed enough to be helpful they need far more space than a book of this scope can afford. Where brands matter, we've specified, but otherwise we suggest you do what we do: Start with established, old-school brands, learn the recipes, and then see what happens when you make substitutions.

The same principle guides how the book is arranged. After a quick look at the DNA that lies behind most of the mixed drinks in popular circulation ("The 7 Cocktail Formulas"—okay, some of them aren't cocktails, but let's not quibble), it starts with what we're calling the Classics, which leads to fourteen drinks that are so foundational that you should know them cold—not all of them, mind you, but certainly the ones you're interested in. If you drink old fashioneds, you should know how to roll one up without having to look at a recipe to do it. The same goes for the martini, the Manhattan, the daiquiri—drinks like that. There are no surprises on this list. Well, okay, one surprise: Chatham Artillery Punch, which is in there because it's the most badass large-bore drink we know, and your friends will treat you with respect verging on fear after you've introduced them to it.

Once you get the essentials down, it's on to "The Second Round": thirty-three recipes that spin off of the formulae and techniques you've already mastered. There's no system behind their selection other than the fact that they're all delicious. The same goes, and then some, for the thirty-six drinks we're calling the "The Third Round": These are hardly essential, and some of them are downright odd, but they're all delicious and it's nice to have a sprinkling of them in your repertoire to keep things fresh. And because you have friends and your friends like to drink, we've started the final cocktail section with five big-batch cocktails followed by five tried-and-true (and not too frilly) punch recipes. Add half a dozen of our favorite recipes for things to eat with your drinks and some hangover-purchased advice about drinking from *Esquire*'s writers and editors and you've got *Drink Like a Man*.

A final note on those drinks. We've pulled them from the pages of *Esquire*. Some are old, dating back to the 1930s, when the magazine was a pioneer in bringing back intelligent drinking after Prohibition. Some are new, from the last decade or so, when *Esquire* worked hard to fix things after the Slow Comfortable Screw Up Against the Wall era. We've tested all of them, but that doesn't necessarily mean you're going to like them the way we like them. Don't be afraid to adjust quantities, switch brands, take liberties. You're the one who's going to be drinking them. If you come up with something tasty, please let us know.

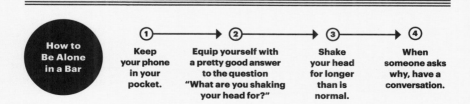

How to Be Alone in a Bar

① Keep your phone in your pocket.

② Equip yourself with a pretty good answer to the question "What are you shaking your head for?"

③ Shake your head for longer than is normal.

④ When someone asks why, have a conversation.

The Only
GEAR
You Actually
Need

For
Cutting

The known universe of bar gear keeps expanding exponentially, and it would be easy to fill your house, garage, office, storage space, and parents' basement with clever new mixing glasses, spoons, ice crackers, shot-layerers, and what have you. Fortunately, most of that stuff is as useful as wings on a hippopotamus. Here's what you'll really need.

Any small, sharp knife will, of course, do; but if you're in the mood to splurge, you can't get a better citrus and garnish knife than the Jackson Cannon bar knife from R. Murphy Knives (rmurphy knives.com). It has an easily controllable tip for fine work—notching orange wheels for your Negronis, for example— and a blade that holds the fruit in place as you pull the knife through it.

For
Cracking
Ice

If you're making mint juleps—and once you make one right, you *will* be making mint juleps—you'll need a mess of ice cracked so fine it's almost powder. The best way to get that is to put ice cubes in a canvas sack (sold these days as a "Lewis Bag," although if you can find coin sacks like the banks use, they're bigger and cheaper), hold the sack closed, and whale the tar out of it with a wood-worker's maul or other large mallet. The bag wicks away the moisture and you're left with fine, dry ice. If you don't have one of these setups handy, you can wrap the ice in a kitchen towel, or any sturdy, clean bit of cloth, and whack it with whatever you've got handy. Or, of course, you can use the crushed ice that the fridge makes, although it won't be nearly as fine as the hand-whacked stuff.

For
Juicing

The Chef'n FreshForce citrus juicer is quick and durable and, due to its gear action, extracts more juice than other hand juicers. If you find yourself making a lot of large punches, a stand juicer can come in handy. You want one with a straight lever action, not one of the geared ones. The Bugatti of the category is made in Mexico by Ra Chand.

For
Measuring

Unlike most jiggers, our two favorites from Cock-tail Kingdom (a premier supplier of high-end bar gear, cocktailkingdom .com) are carefully cali-brated and sturdy. With a 2-oz-over-1-oz [60-ml-over-30-ml] and a ¾-oz-over-½-oz [22-ml-over-15-ml] jigger, you can quickly measure virtually any quantity needed—that is, as long as you can recall your fourth-grade fractions.

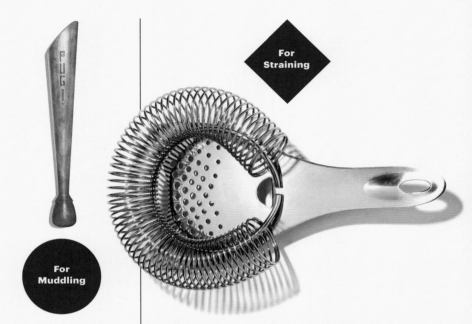

For Straining

For Muddling

For Making Punch

Chris Gallagher's handmade hardwood PUG! muddlers have been the serious bartender's choice for a decade. The cherrywood one is our favorite. There are plenty of other fine muddlers, though. In general, we prefer wood to plastic, but that wood should be unvarnished, sturdy, and weighty. The muddler doesn't have to be huge, but it shouldn't be tiny, either (we draw no parallels). It should have a flat bottom so that things can't lurk unmuddled at the edges of the glass.

A mixing glass demands a strainer. Cocktail Kingdom's julep strainer—the kind that is traditional for stirred drinks and mixing glasses—is a close replica of those in general use before Prohibition and works like the classic it is. Shaken cocktails require a Hawthorne strainer. The one from Modern Mixologist, designed by master bartender Tony Abou-Ganim, fits the bill admirably, as does the Koriko version from Cocktail Kingdom, designed by drinks wizard Don Lee. In general, you want a sturdy strainer with a tightly wound spring.

You'll need a bowl. For four to six people, it should hold 1 gl [3.8 L]. For ten to twelve, 2 gl [7.6 L]. For more, 5 gl [19 L]. It doesn't have to be fancy, but plastic is maybe a bit too unfancy. You'll also need a ladle. Silver is best, of course. Plastic is worst. Glass is okay, but be careful.

For Shaking

For Stirring

For stirred cocktails, many modern bartenders have abandoned the old pint glass in favor of the Japanese-style mixing glass, a sturdy, wide-bottomed glass with a pouring spout molded in. The wide bottom makes it easier to push the ice around with your spoon, and the spout keeps liquid from running down the outside of the glass. The seamless Asanoha from Cocktail Kingdom is our favorite, but the cheaper Yarai also works just fine. You'll also need a barspoon, which is a long-handled, sturdy spoon with a small head. Modern Mixologist's version of the classic barspoon is functional, well balanced, and long enough to get some leverage.

For shaken cocktails, you've got three choices. There's the three-piece shaker, a tin with a cap that has a built-in strainer with its own little cap. We don't recommend these; the little strainer tends to get jammed with ice, the little cap tends to go astray, and sometimes the vacuum the ice creates can make the whole thing impossible to open. Another option and what most bartenders use is the venerable "Boston"-style shaker. In years past, this consisted of a stainless-steel mixing tin jammed down on top of a pint glass, but most bartenders these days replace the glass with a smaller tin. Cheap, effective, and simple. The best shakers—and the industry standards—are Japanese Koriko tins (small and large), available from Cocktail Kingdom. Build the drink in the small tin, add ice, clap the large one over it upside-down, and shake away. With a Boston shaker and Koriko tins, you'll need to supply your own Hawthorne strainer—the kind with a spring (see For Straining, facing page, for recommendations).

Crucial
FOODSTUFFS

A short list of nonperishables
to always have on hand

CAYENNE PEPPER

The most underrated
cocktail garnish.

DEMERARA SUGAR

Tastier and richer
than white sugar.

**LUXARDO
CHERRIES**

The best kind of cherry
to put in a drink.

SIMPLE SYRUP

See Sweetening,
page 21.

WHOLE NUTMEG

A scattering of fresh-grated nutmeg makes a
wonderful garnish for rum drinks and brandy drinks
and is essential for old-school punches. Of course,
that means you'll need a grater, which you can
find in any housewares section (in the absence of
any truly excellent ones, we'll say get what you
like, as long as it's not the Microplane style, which
turns the woody nutmeg into a thousand tiny razor
blades—not what you want to take internally). If you'd
prefer to use the nutmeg that comes preground,
save yourself some money and scrape a tablespoon
or two of dust out of the corner of your garage.
It will taste the same.

How to Discreetly Weep

①
Order martini.

②
Say that you forgot
you were allergic
to vermouth.
"Damn vermouth."

③
Weep.

◆ OR ◆

①
Order martini.

②
Spill martini
on your face so
that tears are
masked by gin.

③
Weep.

◆ OR ◆

①
Order martini.

②
Bring tablet computer
extremely close to
face. "Checking my
e-mails."

③
Weep.

ESSENTIAL TECHNIQUES

and a Few Seemingly Fussy Things That Are Actually

Worth It

Even if you like to drink cocktails, you can live a long, happy life without knowing how to mix them. That's why God gave us bartenders, after all. But if you want to mix your own drinks, it's better to learn how to do it well than to cowboy it and hope things turn out okay.

It helps that the techniques are easy. What makes top bartenders great isn't that they're better at mixing drinks, but that they're better at mixing people—at managing crowds and so forth. But you don't have to worry about that, and after making a few drinks using the following fundamentals, you won't have to worry about mixing drinks, either.

Preparing Ice

Stirred drinks are much colder if you crack the ice first (in shaken drinks, the cracking happens naturally). For a drink or two, cup one ice cube at a time in your left hand and thwack it sharply with the bowl of a long-handled barspoon or—yet another bar gadget here—a flexible-handled ice-tapper. To crack a lot of ice, or for drinks or drinkers that require a more finely cracked grade of ice, put the cubes in a Lewis Bag (see For Cracking Ice, page 15) and brutalize them with a wooden mallet, a skillet, a flat rock—anything that will do the job.

If you plan on making a big bowl of punch that will be sitting out for a while, you'll need a large block of ice. The best way to obtain one of these is to exchange money for it: Many ice companies sell blocks of various sizes. If that's not an option and you're making, say, 5 gl [19 L] of punch or less, you can make your own block by filling a bowl with water and putting it in the freezer for 48 hours. A stainless-steel bowl is best but not essential. For 1 gl [3.8 L] of punch, you'll need a 1-qt [960-ml] bowl; for 5 gl [19 L], a 1-gl [3.8-L] bowl. To get the ice out of the bowl, hold it inverted under the hot-water tap with your fingers overlapping the rim of the bowl; the ice will drop onto your fingers.

Chilling and Warming Glassware

Straight-up drinks such as cocktails stay cold significantly longer in a chilled glass. Simply put the glass in the freezer for 5 minutes or so (the thinner the glass, the quicker it will chill). When that's not possible, fill it with cracked ice and let it sit for a few minutes. Conversely, for your hot drinks, you'll need to warm your mugs. Pour 1 to 2 in [2.5 to 5 cm] of boiling water into the mug, swirl it around until you feel the mug grow warm, and pour it out. Then, as quickly as possible, fill the mug with your drink.

Frosting the Rim of a Glass

A sugar- or salt-rimmed glass is a key component of certain cocktails, serving—much like the twist does—as both garnish and an essential component of the drink. Fortunately, this bit of fanciness is quick and easy to execute. Cut a lemon or lime wheel ½ in [12 mm] thick and then cut out a quarter of it. Grasp that quarter by the rind and run one of the juicy sides of the triangle around the outer rim of the glass. You should have a ½-in [12-mm] wet stripe all the way around the glass. Then hold the glass sideways and slowly roll the wet stripe in a dish of sugar or salt. Put the glass in the freezer to chill. Done. (Some bartenders like to rim only half the glass, in case the customer prefers theirs without; you can do that, or you can simply ask.)

Measuring

We prefer real jiggers over those slant-sided measuring cups you have to peer into to see the quantity. To make jiggers work, you have to do two things: One, memorize how much each holds. That takes all of a minute. Two, use the jigger that exactly holds the quantity you need and fill it right up to surface tension. Then you pour it into your glass and proceed. Simple.

Muddling

Muddling is easy and intuitive. Just make sure the flat end of the muddler is in the glass and press. Some ingredients can be muddled without a muddler; a vigorous shake with cubed ice will often do all the muddling that things like orange slices, raspberries, blackberries, and other soft fruits will need.

Sweetening

Shaking

Stirring (or Stirring Well)

Bartenders commonly sweeten their drinks with sugar syrup, known as "simple syrup" or "rich simple syrup." Make simple syrup by dissolving 1 cup [200 g] granulated sugar in 1 cup [240 ml] water in a small saucepan over medium-low heat. Set aside to cool. When completely cool, transfer to a glass jar with a tight-fitting lid and store in the refrigerator for up to 1 week. For rich simple, as it's known, use 2 cups [400 g] sugar to 1 cup [240 ml] water. To make that into "rock candy syrup," stir in 1 tsp vanilla extract as the syrup cools.

The variations on simple syrup are myriad. Our favorite is to make a rich simple with Demerara sugar, which yields a syrup with a good hit of sugarcane flavor.

Note, however, that many of the most skilled old-time bartenders eschewed syrup in their sours and other citrus drinks, preferring to stir granulated sugar directly into the citrus juice before adding the other ingredients. In our experience, this makes for a brighter-tasting drink.

Measure the ingredients into the smaller of your two tins. Add ice to fill the tin. Rest the tin on a hard surface and cover it with the larger tin, inverted.

Tap the large tin on the bottom to make sure it's seated. Pick up the assembly and flip it so that the large tin is on the bottom. You want to hold it with your left hand around the large tin and your right spanning the joint between the parts, with your thumb on the bottom of the small tin. This will keep it from accidentally flying off.

Now shake—back and forth or up and down along the vertical axis. Don't copy the guy in the craft cocktail bar with the twisty shake. A straight-ahead, vigorous shake for 10 seconds will do the trick.

Now, with the large tin facing up, crack the shaker open—just push the small tin to the side with your thumb; that should break the vacuum that has formed. Then fit your Hawthorne strainer to the shaker and pour.

Combine the ingredients in your mixing glass and take up your barspoon. Rest the long stem of the spoon in the valley between your thumb and forefinger and then grip it lower down between your forefinger and ring finger. Using your wrist for power and your middle finger to push, slide the spoon counterclockwise around the glass. When you reach twelve o'clock, use your index finger to pull the spoon back around. With practice, this will become second nature.

The twist isn't mere garnish. For Manhattans, martinis, and their ilk, it's an integral part of the drink. To make a classic twist, cut a swatch of lemon or orange peel about 1 in [2.5 cm] long and ½ in [12 mm] wide, cutting very thinly to remove only the colorful oily part and avoid the bitter white pith beneath. Hold the twist over the drink, skin-side down, and, with a quick aggressive pinch, fold the twist in half lengthwise, coating the surface of the drink with fresh, sweet citrus oil. Run the twist along the edge of the glass before dropping it in the drink—or not dropping it in the drink. Some people, God knows why, despise seeing a twist floating in their drink and prefer to discard it once its oil has been expressed. We'll leave it up to you: Throw it in or leave it out as you prefer. If you do decide to throw it in, note that meticulous drink-mixers prefer to make sure it floats in the drink with the skin side up.

To remove the peel of ½ lemon, which you'll need for a Brandy Crusta (page 75), keep the lemon whole, trim off the tip, and, starting at the middle with a very sharp knife or vegetable peeler, carefully spiral your way from the middle to the trimmed end. To attempt a whole lemon for making oleo-saccharum, which is apothecary's Latin for "sugar oil" (bartenders usually shorten it to "oleo"), a key component of certain punches (see below), do the same thing but start peeling at the top.

Oleo-saccharum: Using a vegetable peeler, peel 4 lemons. Put the peels in a 1-pt [480-ml] mason jar and add ¾ cup [150 g] sugar. Seal, shake, and leave overnight, shaking occasionally. If you don't have that much time, 3 to 4 hours in the sun will work fine. The sugar will pull the oil out of the peels, resulting in thoroughly infused sugar, candied peels, and, often, a surprising amount of bright, aromatic oil. To turn this into punch, all you have to do is add ¾ cup [180 ml] freshly squeezed and strained lemon juice, reseal the jar, shake it, and pour it into a bowl with a 750-ml bottle of booze, 1 qt [960 ml] of water, and some ice. But we'll get to that (see page 27).

The
EQUIVALENTS

If you're used to drinking in a faux speakeasy and you find yourself in a, uh, bar...

3 oz [90 ml] ⟶ Some
2 oz [60 ml] ⟶ A little
$10 ⟶ $4
2 minutes to make a drink ⟶ 20 seconds
4 minutes ⟶ Another?
Mixologist ⟶ Bartender
Barkeep ⟶ Bartender
Do you have any questions about the cocktail menu? ⟶ What can I get you?
Alchemy ⟶ Mixing a drink
Line out the door ⟶ Seat at the bar
Hidden entrance ⟶ Door
Back room? ⟶ That's a closet.
Third round ⟶ Buyback
Judging what other people are wearing ⟶ Darts
Challenging ⟶ Skunked
Mezcal ⟶ Tequila
Pappy Van Winkle ⟶ Bourbon
Buffalo Trace ⟶ Bourbon
Woodford Reserve ⟶ Bourbon
Elijah Craig ⟶ Never heard of him. Drink?
Ryes ⟶ Bourbons
Grapefruit bitters ⟶ N/A or, Nah.
Lagunitas pils ⟶ Bud
Fernet-Branca ⟶ No idea what you're talking about.
Ephemera ⟶ Crap on the walls
Opens at 5:30 p.m. ⟶ Opens at 8:30 a.m.
Enthusiast ⟶ Drinker
Bon vivant ⟶ Asshole
Celebrant ⟶ Asshole
Mixophile ⟶ Assholephile
Tasty! ⟶ Good.
Delightful! ⟶ Good.
Transcendent! ⟶ You're cut off.

The Endorsement:

SHOTS

〜〜〜

BY DAVID WONDRICH

Sure, downing a shot is antithetical to a measured appreciation of the distiller's craft, and it has nothing to do with the kind of culinary rush one gets from sipping a well-balanced, arctic-cold cocktail. But I've got to stick up for the shot. Sometimes it's restorative; sometimes it's fortifying. Above all, though, it's social. And there are times, even in the most settled life, when it's good to be a member of the team. Some spirits—good brandy, old whiskey, *añejo* tequila—are wasted in shots. Others—flavored rums and vodkas—are not meant for adult drinking. Here's what's left, the shots we've had and would have again. But only once in any given night. It's the repetition that makes the asshole.

BONDED RYE
100 proof, at least four years old. The shot of shots.

BONDED BOURBON
The shot-of-shots-minus.

CHEAP RYE
Still in there swinging.

CHEAP BOURBON
See above.

BECHEROVKA
With Czechs. If you can switch to beer, do it soon.

WHITE DOG
Trade name for unaged whiskey; best straight from the still. Also called moonshine.

IRISH WHISKEY
Practically engineered for shots. Smooth, mellow, warming.

GENEVER
Served chilled, in a little tulip glass with a short beer back.

VODKA
Straight from the freezer, it's a serious contender.

MEZCAL
Best out of little clay cups—or anything.

TEQUILA
Definitely 100-percent agave, preferably silver.

AQUAVIT
Skoal! Best from the freezer.

FERNET, AVERNA, OR ANY OTHER ITALIAN *AMARO* (LIQUEUR)
Only with bartenders.

OVERPROOF RUM
Very strong and very, very dangerous. Pirate juice.

UNDERPROOF RUM
It's still rum.

ALMOST ANY OTHER RUM
See above.

MOUTAI
Only in China, with Chinese people. Then, bring it on.

PISCO
Peruvian with Peruvians, Chilean with Chileans. Don't mix 'em up.

RAKI
With Turks.

GRAPPA
Never again. If it's good, it's worth sipping. If not. [shudder].

The 7 | Cocktail

If you were to feed all the cocktail books ever written into a machine that would grind them down and spit out all the recipes they contain, arranged by ingredients, proportions, and techniques, you'd find that ultimately there aren't that many different ways to turn liquor into something not just palatable, but delicious.

The (Simple) Sour Pattern

↓

This adaptation of the ancient punch pattern goes back to the 1850s.

¾ oz [22 ml] freshly squeezed lemon or lime juice

+

1 tsp superfine sugar

+

2 oz [60 ml] liquor

Combine the citrus juice and sugar in a cocktail shaker, stir briefly, add the liquor and ice cubes and shake well. Strain into a chilled cocktail glass.

The Old Fashioned

↓

Over 200 years old and still one of the simplest and best ways to transform straight booze into cocktail bliss.

½ to 1 tsp sugar

+

3 or 4 dashes bitters

+

2 oz [60 ml] liquor

In an old-fashioned glass, muddle the sugar and bitters with 1 tsp water. Add ice cubes and the liquor and stir. Finish with a lemon or orange twist.

The Margarita/ Sidecar

↓

The sour, sweetened with a liqueur. The variations are endless.

1½ oz [45 ml] liquor

+

¾ oz [22 ml] fruit liqueur

+

½ to ¾ oz [15 to 22 ml] freshly squeezed lime or lemon juice

In a mixing glass or cocktail shaker filled with ice, stir or shake all of the ingredients well. Strain into a chilled cocktail glass.

The Martini/ Manhattan

↓

The preeminent pattern from 1880 on, and one of the most foolproof.

～～～～

2 oz [60 ml] liquor

+

1 oz [30 ml] vermouth or other fortified wine

+

2 or 3 dashes bitters

+

1 tsp liqueur (optional)

═══════

In a mixing glass or cocktail shaker filled with ice, stir all of the ingredients well. Strain into a chilled cocktail glass. Finish with a lemon or orange twist.

The Punch

↓

In no category are the historical proportions more variable. Nonetheless, this 400-year-old pattern is the trunk from which all other modern mixed drinks spring.

～～～～

¾ cup [150 g] sugar infused with the thin-cut peels of 4 whole lemons (see Oleo-saccharum, page 22)

+

¾ cup [180 ml] freshly squeezed lemon or lime juice

+

one 750-ml bottle liquor

+

1 qt [960 ml] water, seltzer water, or club soda

═══════

In a punch bowl, combine the infused sugar with the citrus juice and stir to help dissolve. Add the liquor and water and a large block of ice. Grate nutmeg over the top.

The Toddy

↓

Straightforward and, in a cold climate, indispensable.

～～～～

2 oz [60 ml] boiling water (+ more for heating the mug)

+

1 tsp Demerara sugar

+

2 oz [60 ml] dark spirits

+

1 lemon twist

═══════

Rinse a mug with boiling water. Add the sugar and 1 oz [30 ml] boiling water to the warmed mug. Stir to dissolve the sugar. Add the spirits, lemon twist, and remaining 1 oz [30 ml] boiling water and stir.

The Stinger/ Rusty Nail

→

Liquor, cut with liqueur. Agriculturally simple and very, very strong.

2¼ oz [68 ml] liquor

+

¾ oz [22 ml] herbal liqueur

Stir or shake the liquor and liqueur well with ice cubes in a mixing glass or cocktail shaker and strain into a chilled cocktail glass, or serve on the rocks.

A

LETTER

to a Young

Drinker

~~~

BY TOM CHIARELLA

Look, **drinking is** pretty damned fun. This must be said. Yes. People look better. The ocean looks bluer. We know. And your jokes? Way better, right? Man, laughs are just way better. I mean, right? You just start to like where you are, no matter where that is. It can make you good with the world. And this really can be a good thing. Seriously.

When you start, drinking is all about expansion, escape, getting out. The act feels transgressive, edgy, puissant. You stand on the fringe of some piece of adolescent geography—a parking lot, a quarry, the roof of a rattletrap garage—and furtively take a pull of brandy; you hit the leftover Champagne glasses at a cousin's wedding; creep to the attic with filched bourbon or a backpack loaded with beers long forgotten on the top shelf of some garage refrigerator. This, in turn, forces you into some iconic poses—leaning against the hood of a car, hitting on a 40, throwing back a shot like you were born doing it, levering a beer bottle with two fingers.

When you look back on your world with some booze in you—at your family, at your home, at your troubles—you'll find yourself a little unhinged from expectation, from fear. This is undeniably heady. For a while, for a long while maybe, you surprise yourself. You're braver. Sharper. You say some shit you shouldn't. You say some things that must be said. You sing better. You tell more truths. Things seem to get done when you drink. You feel located in the moment and the moment is all that matters. It feels good out there, beyond the rules, beyond the hand-me-down lessons of school and work, and yes, you'll take another pull.

Understand, from the get-go, these are fun illusions.

The young drinker is usually not self-aware. Observe yourself and take notes. That's a key to drinking: Don't stop looking. When you are less drunk than everyone else, look around. When you are more drunk than anyone else, look at your own dumb ass in the mirror. To persist, you must make a style out of it. Don't slouch. Don't slosh. Make rules: Don't drink beer from boots. Don't chug. Don't shotgun. Don't hoot. Like that. Walk into a bar as if you've been there before. When entering a crowded joint, know your poison. Order simply and clearly. If the bar is uncrowded, if the bartender is smart and attentive, ask for recommendations. Draft your own lessons. Learn from your mistakes. Quickly. You're allowed a couple when you start. After that, it's on you.

Lose the urgency, too. Drinking should not be the event in itself.

There is no lesson plan, but you have to learn. No authoritative how-to.

That's your job. Everyone in a bar is a kind of how-to. How to handle it, how to share it, and how to let it go. Drinking must be mastered, or it will master you.

Every once in a while, you'll turn around and you'll encounter that guy, any one of many guys, really—the shouter, the stumbler, the puncher, the teary guy, the sleepy drunk, the ass-grabber, the chest-poker, the jabber-mouth, the spitter, the wobbly fool. One version or another, he's always there. Really look then. Understand that that guy doesn't know what he is, doesn't know what he looks like, what people say about him. Fair warning: You'll probably be every one of those guys eventually. Figure out that you don't have to be.

Quit. For some period of time, anyway. A week. A month. Three years. Whatever it takes. Just walk away. Study the absence. Feel it. In some ways, you'll find you're right back on the outside. Know what it means to not drink, too.

Start again if you want. Be better at it this time.

Eventually, you'll have your patterns of control and eccentricity. Some of this is luck, some of it persistence.

At some point, you'll drink only gin in the summer, whiskey all winter. Or you'll make batches of cocktails for friends. You'll buy rounds, for the women at the jukebox, for the whole goddamned place. You'll stock your own bar and reconsider olives, cocktail onions, and the importance of limes. You'll have a good bottle of whiskey in your desk drawer at work so long that you'll forget it's there. And some bartender, somewhere, will work your drink the minute you tug your way in. You'll make one brief, well-considered toast a year, though people will ask for more. You'll have your own philosophy about the relative harmlessness of mixing liquors, about why you order a beer behind your shot, about drinking at the beach.

When asked, you'll offer this stuff up. Young drinkers need to know. And the music in the bar will rise, inflating the circus tent of the evening once more. Then your round arrives. That menagerie of clinking highballs. Nice. Maybe then you'll look over the shoulders of the young drinkers or at the ocean. That's when you'll say, because of it all and despite it all: Drinking is pretty damn good.

The
STAGES
of
Drinking

One
Drink

BY ROSS McCAMMON

The thing about one drink—a glass of liquor we're talking about, hopefully a stiff pour—is that it doesn't involve enough alcohol to make anything stop working. Your eyesight, your natural grace, your moral compass—they're all left intact. Because one drink doesn't compromise anything. It enhances. You have one drink and your world becomes slightly better. The bar is a slightly better bar. Your dog is a slightly better dog. Your work is slightly more brilliant. And for that, you pay no price. Your outward appearance is unchanged—to your drinking partner, to your boss, to your kid, to a cop. You haven't wrecked anything. You haven't said anything stupid. You were a gentleman when you started drinking and you are a gentleman—a slightly more interesting one, which is nice—when you finish drinking. For a good thirty minutes (it doesn't work if you don't sip the drink and make it last), everything about the universe is slightly less intolerable. One drink is a free ride.

Two Drinks

BY DAVID GRANGER

Here's what two drinks is: When you go in for your physical and you make the mistake of asking your doctor about drinking, he'll say, "Two drinks a day is fine." And he'll say it in a curt but friendly way that suggests that for any normal, well-adjusted man without a tendency toward dependency or maybe a serious problem with alcohol, two drinks is plenty, two drinks is more than you actually need, but he's being a nice guy. To his mind, two drinks is reasonable.

Here's what else two drinks is. Two drinks is 7:15. Two drinks is four or five hours till bed. Two drinks is, to put it another way, a glow that needs to be carefully tended to keep it from (a) descending into headache or (b) accelerating out of control.

Two drinks is an opportunity. It's the chance to manage your elevated state of mind into one of the better nights of your life.

Two drinks is a beginning—the start of a progression from just right on through excellent and then on, toward the end of the night, to satisfied. But two drinks is by no means an end point. And your primary caregiver needs to realize that.

Three Drinks

BY RYAN D'AGOSTINO

Empirically, there is no better number of drinks than three. Three drinks shoves you right up to the blurry border between you and drunkenness, a line in the sand that's been washed over by a wave—you can still see it, but barely. It's a thrilling place to be. You're flying, feeling it, maybe spitting out the wrong word every now and then, maybe calling your sister for no reason, but you could still operate a forklift if you really had to. You can still hit the dartboard. One fewer and you're drinking responsibly; one more and you're walking on your knees and suggesting everybody go for karaoke.

The important thing is, you're having the time of your life, but there's no danger of missing the urinal when you take a leak. You feel fantastic, your cares have dissolved, and everyone is interesting. Every conversation is both funny and important. Good ideas seem brilliant. Semi-interesting theories fascinate. Plans are made, and they sound like fun. And if, at the end of the night, you get in a taxi and it goes the wrong way and you're not exactly sure where you're headed, everything will end up okay.

Four Drinks

BY CHRIS JONES

Drinking a fourth drink dictates that a certain kind of evening is about to unfold—namely, one in which you will be drunk. Because nobody stops at four drinks. Four is to inebriation what the St. Louis arch is to the West: It's the gateway drink, the point of no return. A fourth empty glass or bottle or mason jar set on the bar or table or broken in the hobo fire in front of you is your announcement to the rest of the world that, at some point in the next twelve to twenty-four hours, you will be left trying very hard to remember or even harder to forget.

There's no shame in that, of course. But there is shame—a great and insidious shame, a shame that won't be washed off by a thousand iodine showers—in denying what it is you're up to. Sack up. None of this "One more and I'll call it a night" blah-blah. Nobody's fooling anybody here. Especially after you've settled into old Number Four. You're a man for whom sobriety is no longer an option.

But a brave new world has opened up for you, a great blinding universe of magic and possibility. You're a man who might start confusing nouns with verbs. You're a man who might fall off his barstool. You're a man who might sleep on the floor in his clothes.

The Endorsement:

TONIC AND BITTERS

BY JOHN KENNEY

Maybe you're running a 10K tomorrow. Or you're on painkillers. Or maybe you just need a breather. And yet circumstances have conspired to put you at a bar, and you want *something*. To your credit, you can't bring yourself to ask for a Diet Pepsi. So what do you do? You call a tonic and bitters—three or four dashes Angostura bitters in an ice-filled glass, tonic water to the top, and a wedge of lime. It's a stomach settler, if that's what's wanted—as cool and soothing as that first sip of ginger ale you took as a kid with a stomach virus. But more than that, it feels like you're having a drink. It's a little sharp, not sweet. Crisp. Bracing, even. It tastes just like a good drink, only without the booze. Which is exactly what it is.

The Drinks

(and a little food)

THE CLASSICS

14 Drinks Every Man Should Know How to Make

The Endorsement:

THE WEAK DRINK

BY TOM CHIARELLA

When I was sixteen, I yanked open the door of Jim Miller's Bar in Rochester, New York, walked to the bar, and calmly ordered a gin and tonic in the middle of one summer afternoon. The bartender smirked, gave me a short pour of well gin in a tall glass, shot it with tonic water to the brim, then set it in front of me like an offering plate. No lime. When I picked it up, he told me to get lost after it was done. An hour later, having outlived the dirty looks, having watched the better part of an episode of *General Hospital* in the presence of neighbors I never knew I had, I'd sucked it dry, chewed each piece of ice into oblivion. I left the glass dead empty, gave the bartender a purposeless wave, and walked out into the rain. Outside, I realized that

I was not the least bit drunk. I felt like I'd been bilked. Next time, I told myself, I would order a double.

In many ways, that's what I did for the next thirty years, insisting on those doubles, always looking for the long pour, the stiff highball, operating perpetually under the adolescent supposition that drinking in bars was a kind of value equation, a contest won by finding a bartender who gave you more booze for the same money. But somewhere in there, I discovered the functional, foundational pleasure of a weak drink.

This does not mean bad drinks. Classic cocktails fall out of the equation; there's no such thing as a weak old fashioned. Just a lousy one. Nor do I try to undo the chemistry of a house specialty; asking for a "weak" pineapple-melon

Mojito in a boutique hotel bar sounds, well, weak. Like any drinker, I want exactly what I ask for, specifically made for me. And getting a weak drink demands a clarity that good bartenders appreciate.

Particular orders work better. "A pint glass," I say. "A lot of tonic, two limes, and just a little vodka on top."

The drink is good only if the terms are clear. There is no fear in the order. I lock eyes with the bartender, ask for a single in a highball or a short pour in a pint glass. I ask for a lot of ice. A bartender never cares what you order, just that you order.

"Make it weak," I say. "Take care of me." The last part is the trick; I've learned that's all I should have ever wanted from a bar.

Old Fashioned

The old fashioned (invented circa 1800, christened circa 1880) is the Fender Strat of cocktails: It embodies the classic American combination of offhand style, swagger, and micrometer engineering. And it's simple enough that anyone can make it, yet sophisticated enough that you never get tired of it. It can be applied equally well to speed-rail bourbon and Cordon Bleu cognac, taming the one and coddling the other. It sips slow and easy when you need that, and goes down like a fireball when you don't. The ingredients are cheap and readily available, and you can leave everything but the lemon on a shelf without worrying about spoilage (and the lemon is dispensable). In the fullness of time, some people have come to believe that the "old-fashioned" way of making an old fashioned includes mashing slices of fruit into it—or even, God forbid, maraschino cherries—and drowning the whole sticky mess with club soda. Those people might call such a thing an old fashioned, but that's not an old fashioned. This is.

To Make

Place **½ tsp sugar** in the bottom of an old-fashioned glass.

Add **2 or 3 healthy dashes Angostura bitters** and **1 tsp water**. Muddle to dissolve the sugar.

Add **3 ice cubes** to the glass. Stir.

Add **2 oz [60 ml] straight rye whiskey** or bourbon whiskey. Stir again.

Twist **a swatch of thin-cut lemon or orange peel** over the top, and drop it in. Let sit for 1 minute, then serve.

Makes 1 drink

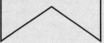

A LITTLE ILLUMINATION,

If We May

Because the old fashioned is the most fundamental of cocktails, we'd like to expound on the fundamentals of the old fashioned.

THE TWIST

This is not a garnish. The dose of lemon or orange oil that you spray on the surface of the drink is the appetizer to the booze's main course.

THE WATER

Dissolves the sugar, without seriously diluting the liquor. That's the ice's job.

THE WHISKEY

Let it be American and bonded (that is, at least four years old, and 100 proof) and not too expensive.

THE SUGAR

It's less to make the drink sweet than to give back the texture the melting ice is taking away.

THE ICE

Try a mix of a little cracked ice for fast dilution and a couple of large, slow-melting cubes to keep it stable as you sip it.

THE BITTERS

The pungent, volatile spice of the bitters briefly masks the top notes of the liquor, so we process it as a cocktail, not a glass of whiskey.

THE GLASS

The standard rocks glass used by American bars these days is technically a double old-fashioned glass. You don't want that. You want the single old-fashioned glass, which holds 5 to 6 oz [150 to 180 ml] and won't make a healthy 2 oz [60 ml] of booze look like half a drink.

no.
2

Manhattan

The venerable old Manhattan—it first appeared in print in New York in 1882—worked as the Default American Cocktail for so many years because it's so simple. The Manhattan, although simple, is not quite that simple; not including the garnish, there are three ingredients, not two, and adding a little more or a little less of any one of them changes everything. A properly built Manhattan can be every bit as good as a good martini (as heretical and blasphemous as that may sound to cocktail dogmatists of the old school), bold and fortifying, yet as relaxing as a deep massage. A bad Manhattan will always be much worse, either sticky-sweet or a harsh bucket of slightly adulterated whiskey.

That proper building requires rye whiskey decently aged (at least four years) and at around 100 proof. Failing that, it's better to use a 100-proof bourbon than an 80-proof rye, and an 80-proof rye than an 80-proof bourbon. Rye is spicy and lean and demands a goodly slug of vermouth. We prefer two parts whiskey to one of vermouth, but equal parts—as they made them at the old Manhattan Club—also has its charms, as does three parts whiskey to one of vermouth. Any less vermouth than that and the drink suddenly goes from a harmonious blend to badly adulterated whiskey. And don't forget the bitters. They tie the other ingredients together and are no more optional than mortar is in laying bricks.

In a mixing glass, combine **2 oz [60 ml] rye, 1 oz [30 ml] sweet vermouth**, and **2 dashes Angostura bitters** with **cracked ice** and stir well. (Some prefer to shake their Manhattans. There's nothing wrong with that, really—at least no more than putting ketchup on a hot dog is wrong. If you like your Manhattan cloudy and topped with an algae-like foam, shake away. It won't taste any worse, anyway, although it'll feel thinner on the tongue.)

Strain into a chilled cocktail glass and finish with **a swatch of lemon peel** or, of course, garnish with **a maraschino cherry** (which is subject to the same challenge [re: purity] as adding an olive to a martini).

Makes 1 drink

ADULTERATIONS

SUBSTITUTES FOR VERMOUTH

• **Dubonnet** or **Lillet**. Wine-based aperitifs and the like can work fine, but must be approved on a case-by-case basis.

• **Ruby port** is nice.

• So are **Italian amari**.

• **Madeiras and the sweeter sherries** (not a fino, manzanilla, or amontillado).

• 1 tsp **smoky Scotch** to rinse the glass before pouring the drink into it.

NOTE: *You occasionally see a "Perfect Manhattan" on a cocktail menu. In drink-making, "perfect" always refers to the addition of equal parts sweet and dry vermouth. We can't recommend it. We find that dry vermouth clashes with the whiskey and makes an awkward drink; you may disagree.*

To Make

Fill a mixing glass with **cracked ice**.

↓

Pour in **½ oz [15 ml] dry vermouth** (we prefer Noilly Prat), stir briefly, and strain out).

↓

Add **2 ½ oz [75 ml] gin** (we prefer Tanqueray, Beefeater, Junipero, or Hendrick's)—you want the gin to be around 94 proof.

↓

Stir briskly for about 10 seconds, strain into a chilled cocktail glass, and garnish with **an olive**.

Makes 1 drink

Martini

In the 1800s, it went something like this: Two parts, or even one part, gin to one part sweet vermouth with an extra dash of simple syrup and a hit of bitters. Garnish: Twist of lemon peel. The dry martini—dry vermouth, dash of orange bitters, and no syrup—was a critter of the Gilded Age, coming in around 1895. Proportions were still seldom more aggressive than two-to-one. By the '30s, though, we find the Stork Club pouring 'em at (an entirely reasonable) five parts gin to one part vermouth. At the height of the martini's powers, in the gray-flannel-suit years, the "see-through" went something like eight parts gin to no parts vermouth, with an olive.

We've done extensive testing, which has taught us that within the evolution, the 1800s iteration is a most pleasant tipple, if not exactly what is invoked by the word "martini" in most people's minds; the 1890s one is a most civilized drink, if you have good vermouth. The Stork Club version is the liquid equivalent of Philip Johnson's Seagram Building: bold, seamless, elegant. (The "see-through"? Merely iced gin—which is how, if that's what you want, you should have the courage to order it.)

To Make

In a mixing glass, combine **1½ oz [45 ml] London dry gin**, **¾ oz [22 ml] Campari**, and **¾ oz [22 ml] sweet vermouth** (like Martini & Rossi or Carpano Antica) with **cracked ice** and stir well.

Strain into a chilled cocktail glass and garnish with **a swatch of orange peel**. (This is the American way of making the drink, which works wonderfully as a predinner cocktail. To be truly Italian, build it on the rocks with 1 oz [30 ml] each of gin, vermouth, and Campari; top it off with a splash of chilled soda water; and garnish with half an orange wheel. You can drink those all afternoon.)

Makes 1 drink

no.
4

Negroni

The Italians, as a rule, are not drinkers—at least, not as the Anglo-Saxon understands the term. It's not that inhabitants of the Boot avoid the stuff; they just don't consider it sufficient recreation unto itself. Alcohol goes *with* things; it's never the focus of the evening.

That attitude could make for forgettable drinks. Luckily, there's Campari. Campari has associations. Summer-weight suits with narrow lapels, Ray-Ban Wayfarers, Vespas, brown-eyed blonde women in Capri pants. *La dolce vita.* A violently red, bittered-up 48-proof tonic doesn't sound like much to build a cocktail culture on, but somehow it works. In fact, combined with gin and Italian vermouth, it makes a Negroni, which is one of the world's indispensable cocktails.

To Make

In a very large highball, Collins glass, or tumbler, preferably 24 oz [720 ml], combine **1½ oz [45 ml] freshly squeezed lemon juice** and **1 tsp superfine sugar**. Stir to dissolve the sugar.

Add **3 oz [90 ml] gin** (Hendrick's is particularly cooling).

Fill the glass with the largest **ice cubes** you can fit.

Add **seltzer water** to within 1 in [2.5 cm] of the rim.

Garnish, if you like, with a "flag"— **a maraschino cherry pinned to a slice of orange** with a toothpick or small skewer.

Makes 1 drink

no.
5

Tom Collins

This simple, refreshing mix of lemon juice, sugar, gin, and seltzer has been around for at least a century and a half. Nevertheless, it's become one of those things that everyone is acquainted with but nobody actually pays close attention to. Make it a double, though (like this recipe), in a big glass tumbler, and suddenly, for no reason known to science, it's better, more vibrant, alive. Or maybe having more booze in your hand just makes you think it is.

In a cocktail shaker, stir **½ to 1 tsp superfine sugar** and **½ oz [15 ml] freshly squeezed lime juice**.

Add **2 oz [60 ml] flavorful white rum**, such as Havana Club three-year-old (if you can get it), Banks 5 Island, Owney's, or Plantation 3 Stars.

Fill the shaker with **ice** and shake well.

Strain into a chilled cocktail glass.

Makes 1 drink

no.
6

Daiquiri

Many have claimed credit for the daiquiri—Cuban barmen, American mining engineers, German princelings, what have you. But rum and lime have a long history together. The British navy began administering lime juice to the ranks in 1795. Could it have been long before the swabbies started mixing it with their daily rum ration? And most Caribbean and South American peoples make liquor out of sugarcane, grow limes, and drink them together. What's the Brazilian Caipirinha but a daiquiri on the rocks? In fact, the daiquiri represents such an obvious marriage between local ingredients (rum, sugar, limes) and American technology (cocktail shaker, ice) that it would take the chowder-headedest duffer who ever buttoned a trouser *not* to invent it.

Note on the rum: Some prefer dark over white; if you do use dark rum, cut back a little on the sugar.

To Make

In a cocktail shaker, combine **1½ oz [45 ml] silver tequila*, ¾ oz [22 ml] Cointreau**,** and **¾ oz [22 ml] freshly squeezed lime juice** with **ice** and shake well.

Strain into the prepared cocktail glass.

Makes 1 drink

* The tequila should be 100-percent agave, the plant from which the stuff is traditionally made. Save the great golden *añejos* for sipping.

** The Cointreau yields results clearly superior to Triple Sec, most brands of which are marred by an unpleasant chemical aftertaste.

no.
7

Margarita

Although the margarita's roots are deep—it was around in the '40s—the margarita is really a child of the '70s. *Esquire*'s revised *Handbook for Hosts* (published in 1973) lists it among the "twelve most useful of all drinks."

Essentially a variation on the sidecar—substituting tequila for brandy, lime juice for lemon, and salt rim for sugar—the margarita shares its characteristic luminosity and, especially, its sneakiness. Yet it's a completely different drink, less plush than the sidecar but more dignified (when properly made, of course, without strawberries and such gratuitous cargo).

no.
8

Whiskey Sour

In a cocktail shaker, stir together a level **1 tsp superfine sugar** and **¾ oz [22 ml] freshly squeezed lemon juice**. (It's easier to dissolve the sugar without the booze.)

Add **2 oz [60 ml] American whiskey** of any kind.

Fill the shaker with **ice**, shake like a jackhammer operator, and strain into a chilled cocktail glass.

↓

Garnish with **a maraschino cherry**. Drink. Repeat. (For a New York sour, float **½ oz [15 ml] dry red wine** on top of the finished sour by pouring it gently from a small cruet or vial onto the back of a spoon held just over the surface of the drink. The astringency of the wine sets off the whiskey beautifully and the look of the thing is irresistible.)

Makes 1 drink

No drink formula could be simpler: Booze, lemon or lime juice, and sweetener. Done. And none has given us so much; the whiskey sour, the daiquiri, the Collins, even the sidecar and the margarita—all sours. And none can be so awful; either tooth-strippingly tart or candy-sweet instead of what it's supposed to be, which is dry and complex.

Now, we don't want to make balancing a sour sound like molecular biology. But the sour is machined to a finer tolerance than other drinks, so it takes a little management. Although most bartenders these days balance out the citrus with simple syrup, what you want to use here is fine-ground granulated sugar, like the old masters of the bar used to insist on. A drink with sugar stirred into lemon juice is clean and vibrant. A modern drink with, say, ¾ oz [22 ml] each of citrus juice and syrup has a slick, almost plastic texture. (If the ratio here seems too tart for your taste, better to pull the citrus back to ½ oz [15 ml] than to increase the sugar. That stuff will kill you.)

no.
9

Mint Julep

Dating back to at least 1770, the julep is the oldest American drink. In its early years, it was primarily made with brandy, the more expensive the better, often with port, sherry, or Madeira mixed in. We'll let the experimenters play with those and stick to good old American bourbon here.

Per the Kentucky School of Julepistics: (1) Use a chilled, dry 12- to 14-oz [360- to 420-ml] glass, tall and slim (or better yet, of course, the traditional silver beaker). (2) Crack the ice, then carefully "dry" it; that is, drain off any excess water before putting it in the glass. (3) After the ice is in, don't handle the glass with bare hands, as the touch will kill the frost. Likewise, each julep should be served wrapped in a napkin or small linen doily. (4) The glass will not frost if it's in the wind, if it's wet, if it's filled with undried ice, or when handled. You can sometimes speed the frost by twirling the glass, or by placing it in the coldest part of the refrigerator for about 30 minutes. (5) Use only the freshest mint and, of that, the smallest, most tender leaves. (6) If you use a straw, keep it short so you can get your nose in among the mint. So many rules. . . . But it's worth all that.

To Make

Stir together **2 tsp sugar** and **2 tsp water** in a chilled, dry slim glass or beaker.

Add **5 or 6 fresh mint leaves** and press lightly with a muddler.

Pack the glass with **finely cracked ice.** Pour **3 oz [90 ml] fine, old bourbon** over the ice.

Stir briskly until the glass frosts (be careful not to touch the glass). Add more finely cracked ice and stir again.

Stick **a few sprigs of fresh mint** into the ice so that the partaker will get the aroma, add a couple of straws, and serve.

Makes 1 drink

Still not enough
MINT FLAVOR?

TRY THIS: For each julep, in a small bowl, lightly cover **2 or 3 fresh mint sprigs** with **superfine sugar**, add **1 oz [30 ml] spring water**, muddle, and let stand to macerate for 10 to 15 minutes. Strain through a fine-mesh sieve into the ice-filled glass, then stir in the bourbon as directed.

To Make

Combine
**8 fresh lime
squares** (see
facing page) and
1 tsp sugar in
an old-fashioned
glass or small
tumbler.

↓

Muddle, then
add **3 or 4 ice
cubes**.

↓

Pour in **2 oz
[60 ml] cachaça**.
Stir well and
serve.

Makes 1 drink

no.
10

Caipirinha

Cachaça, the raw sugarcane spirit from which Brazil's
national drink is made, looks like vodka and, at its
cheapest, can taste as if it were aged in old truck tires.
However, even that stuff, the so-called industrial cachaça,
mixed with muddled lime, sugar, and ice, intoxicates
strangely and has an elemental appeal. Artisanal cachaça,
on the other hand, is a pure sugarcane-juice brandy
and as honest and subtle a spirit as is made on Earth.
A Caipirinha made with that is angelic.

THE TRICK

Making a great Caipirinha is all about handling the lime. Here's a particularly effective way.

①
With a sharp paring knife, slice off the ends of a lime, cutting far enough to expose the flesh.

②
Cut the lime in half lengthwise.

③
Make two long cuts that meet in a V to cut out the white, fibrous strand of pith running down the length of the cut side of each half. Try not to cut so deeply that you slice through the rind.

④
Make three deep, evenly spaced cuts perpendicular to the cut where the white part was. This should leave you a lime half scored into eight little squares.

⑤
Drop this in your glass, cut-side up, add the sugar, and muddle.

To Make

In a cocktail shaker, combine **2 oz [60 ml] London dry gin** and ⅔ **oz [20 ml] Rose's lime juice** with **ice** and shake well.

Strain into a chilled cocktail glass and top off with **1 oz [30 ml] chilled club soda.**

Makes 1 drink

no.

11

Gimlet

The gimlet is a drink that formerly enjoyed a huge vogue but now is suffering from the backlash against nonfresh ingredients—in this case, Rose's lime juice. But nonfresh was the point of the original drink; in the British navy, where and when it originated, they did not have fresh limes. The preserved juice was still ripe in vitamin C, if a little odd tasting, and the gimlet was a typical sailor's improvisation based on what was at hand—preserved lime juice, gin, and, originally, it appears, club soda. In fact, the soda is key to balancing out a gimlet to this day; a splash of it helps to tame the sweetness of the Rose's much better than adding extra gin does.

To Make

Rinse a mug
with boiling water
to warm it.

↓

Add **1 tsp raw
sugar, 1 oz
[30 ml] boiling
water**, and **a
longish swatch
of thin-cut lemon
peel** to the mug
and stir briefly.

↓

Add **2 oz [60 ml]
single-malt
Scotch** (Glenlivet
or Glenrothes, if
you like it smooth;
Laphroaig,
Bowmore, or
Ardbeg, if you
like it smoky)
and another **1 oz
[30 ml] boiling
water**. Drink up.

Makes 1 drink

no.
12

Hot Toddy

There are times when the world is awfully—frighteningly, even—cold and dark. When the little flame of life within is guttering in a cold draft, when the spirit drags and the body falters, that's when you need a hot toddy. Nothing else will do. The original version, and simplest one, is the best. The toddy is a noble drink and does not require decadent liqueurs, fruit juice, cider of any kind, or indeed anything beyond good malt whiskey, a little bit of sugar, boiling water (and not too much of it), and perhaps—just perhaps—a strip of lemon peel.

no.
13

Chatham Artillery Punch

The One True Punch to Rule Them All. The credit for this delicious, lethal, and insidious punch goes to Alonzo B. Luce, a Yankee living in Savannah, Georgia, in the 1850s. Many versions exist, but Luce's version has a simple magnificence that none of the others can touch. Be warned, though: Chatham Artillery Punch has a well-earned reputation for laying them low in their dozens and in their hundreds.

To Make

Infuse ¾ **cup [150 g] sugar** with the **peels of 4 lemons** (see Oleo-saccharum, page 22).

Add ¾ **cup [180 ml] freshly squeezed and strained lemon juice** to the jar with the oleo, reseal, and shake until the sugar is dissolved.

Pour the mixture into a 1-gl [3.8-L] punch bowl.

Add **1 cup [240 ml] good bourbon, 1 cup [240 ml] VSOP-grade cognac** or Armagnac, and **1 cup [240 ml] strong, funky Jamaican rum** such as Smith & Cross to the bowl.

Add a **block of ice** made from 1 qt [960 ml] water, stir, and refrigerate for 30 minutes. Before serving, stir in **one 750-ml bottle chilled Champagne** and garnish with thinly sliced **lemon wheels**.

Makes about 20 drinks

Eggnog

It usually comes from a carton—a 0-proof concoction of milk, eggs, high-fructose corn syrup, carrageenan, and artificial flavors. If you're lucky, your host will spike it with Bacardi or cheap bourbon. Even thus industrialized, it's still not a bad drink.

Made fresh, however, eggnog is a whole other story. Less like melted cheap ice cream, more like a drink so wicked, heady, and compelling that it has to be tied tightly to a once-a-year holiday. Sure, it requires a little exercising of the kitchen arts to get together, but it's effort well spent—particularly if you take a cue from the nineteenth century and keep an open mind about the alcohol that goes into it. Bourbon will always work, of course, but the traditional mix of cognac and dark rum makes for a complex, multilayered drink that's hard to refuse. Then again, so does replacing the spirits with sherry, Madeira, tawny port, or a combination thereof for a 'nog just as flavorful as the bourbon or cognac-rum version but far less intoxicating. You can vary the hooch, but the basic recipe stays the same.

To Make

Separate the whites and yolks of **10 eggs**, preferably large organic ones.

↓

In a punch bowl, combine ¾ **to 1 cup [150 to 200 g] sugar** (depending on how sweet you like it) and the egg yolks and whisk until the sugar is dissolved.

↓

Gradually stir in **3 to 5 cups [720 ml to 1.2 L] spirits** (see facing page) and **1 qt [960 ml] organic whole milk**.

↓

In a nonreactive (glass, enamel, or earthenware) bowl, whip the egg whites until they form soft peaks. Gently fold them into the eggnog base. Refrigerate for 1 hour.

↓

Grate **fresh nutmeg** over the top and ladle forth.

Makes about 12 drinks

Egg Nog
TWO WAYS

~~~~~~

CLASSIC EGGNOG
Use **2 cups [480 ml]**
VSOP-grade cognac

+

1 cup [240 ml] rich dark rum

SHERRY EGGNOG
Use **3 cups [720 ml]**
amontillado sherry or **4 cups**
[960 ml] oloroso sherry

+

1 cup [240 ml] fine, rich Madeira

What a
BARTENDER
Should Be

BY DAVID GRANGER

I've begun telling stories about my bartender again. It's been years since I've had a bartender to tell a story about.

We're in the age of the professional bartender now, and it has many benefits. But fostering bartenders with a discernible personality is not generally one of them. The modern bartender is often so engrossed in the complications of his craft or, once the drink is made, in explaining to you the complications of his craft, that he doesn't have the will to be anything more than an artisan. It's complicated being a modern bartender, what with the vests and the tricky facial hair and all the stirring. Bartenders have become more insular, less worldly. They think their sole job is to make (and make and make) drinks.

Which makes my new bartender kind of refreshing. I've been drinking at this place three blocks north. Old place, been around forever. Female bartender. She's, um, truculent. The kind of attractive that has to grow on you. She never seems to notice (or maybe the right word is "care") that I've been there before. On my fourth visit, I asked her if she could make me a Manhattan that had tequila in place of the whiskey. This is what she said, "Um . . . no." (Story!)

Then she relented and made it, reserving a little for herself. She tasted it. This is what she said, "Well, that was a little less disgusting than I expected." (Story!) To be fair, she does talk. She is attentive. She's masterful, she's in charge, she's quick, and she doesn't

bother you unless you want to be bothered.

You go there with a friend or a business associate and she takes your drink order. You talk to your friend and, before you even notice it, your drink is on the bar. I watched her make my Manhattan the other night. She did not labor over it. This is how she made it. She iced a pint glass, filled it two-thirds of the way with rye, threw in some sweet vermouth and some bitters, shook it, let it chill some, then poured it into an oversize martini glass. It tasted like a Manhattan. It was cold.

I think she's warming up to me. The other night I asked her if she could make me a tequila Manhattan.

"Sure," she said. "I'm in a good mood tonight."

THE SECOND ROUND

Slightly Less Essential Cocktails,
but Just as Delicious

Algonquin

It being Prohibition, and lunchtime, there wasn't a lot of drinking at the Round Table. That didn't stop New York's Algonquin Hotel from baptizing several cocktails in its name, for the most part with pretty shaky results (rum, blackberry brandy, and Bénédictine? Nah). This may have been one of 'em, although nobody seems to be sure. In any case, it's fairly unlikely the wits of the Round Table grazed on it, even when they were off-duty. Strictly a highball crowd, as we read them, with the occasional martini. Not a bad drink, though—spicy (although not so much as Dorothy Parker), mellow (although not so much as Robert Benchley), and potent enough that three will enable you to perfect your Harpo Marx imitation. Also, we find that adding 2 or 3 dashes of orange bitters before stirring does wonders for this drink.

In a mixing glass, combine **½ oz [15 ml] rye whiskey**, **¾ oz [22 ml] dry vermouth**, **¾ oz [22 ml] unsweetened pineapple juice**, and **finely cracked ice** and stir well. (Don't shake it. If you do, the pineapple juice will foam.) Strain into a chilled cocktail glass. **MAKES 1 DRINK**

Aviation

A gin drink for people who think they don't like gin, and one of the foundational drinks of the modern cocktail revolution.

In a cocktail shaker, combine **2 oz [60 ml] Plymouth gin**, **¾ oz [22 ml] freshly squeezed lemon juice**, and **2 tsp Luxardo maraschino liqueur** or 1½ tsp maraschino liqueur plus 1 tsp crème de violette with **ice** and shake well. Strain into a chilled cocktail glass. **MAKES 1 DRINK**

Bloody Mary

A glance at the Bloody Mary's component parts—neutral spirits, restorative juices, salts, capsaicins and other volatile oils—indicates that its origins lie in the shadowy world of the hangover cure, and there, as far as *Esquire* is concerned, it may remain, a useful citizen of the Cocktail Republic, to be sure, if not exactly a leading one.

Squeeze the liquid from **1 tsp freshly grated horseradish** into a mixing tin and add **4 oz [120 ml] tomato juice, 2 oz [60 ml] vodka, 1½ tsp freshly squeezed lemon juice, a splash of Worcestershire sauce, 3 or 4 dashes of Tabasco sauce**, and **ice**. Pour gently into a second mixing tin, roll back and forth three or four times, then pour unstrained into a Collins glass. Add a **pinch of salt** and **a grind or two of fresh pepper**. Garnish with **a lemon wedge** or a stalk of celery, if you like. Do not garnish with a cheeseburger on a stick, an order of wings, a whole lobster, or a pizza of any shape or kind. **MAKES 1 DRINK**

Boulevardier

This whiskey-based sibling of the Negroni goes back to Paris in the 1920s. While it lacks the Negroni's incisiveness, it makes up for it by adding a subtle richness to the drink. Make it with rye and you've got not only a sharper drink, but an Old Pal (also from Paris in the '20s).

In a mixing glass, stir **1 oz [30 ml] strong bourbon** or Canadian whisky, **1 oz [30 ml] Campari**, **1 oz [30 ml] red vermouth** with **cracked ice**. Strain into chilled cocktail glass. Garnish with **a swatch of thin-cut orange peel. MAKES 1 DRINK**

Brandy Alexander

The original Alexander, from 1910 or thereabouts, was a weird mix of crème de cacao, cream, and gin. The brandy version must have been invented about .0578 seconds after the gin version was first sipped. Sweet and decadent, but tasty for all that. If you're ever tempted to wear a burgundy velour turtleneck, this is your drink.

In a cocktail shaker, combine **1 oz [30 ml] brandy**, **1 oz [30 ml] crème de cacao**, and **1 oz [30 ml] heavy cream** with **ice** and shake well. Strain into a chilled cocktail glass. **MAKES 1 DRINK**

BRANDY ALEXANDER

Brandy Crusta

This classic drink is the result of bartenders monkeying with the basic "Cock-Tail," the cornerstone of American mixology, which was simply a shot of liquor (any liquor, although they preferred French brandy and Dutch gin) stirred up with a lump of sugar, a squirt or two of bitters, and a generous splash of water. This variation comes from New Orleans saloonkeeper Joseph Santini, circa 1850.

Run **a lemon wedge** around the rim of a chilled cocktail glass, then dip the moist rim in **superfine sugar** and let dry. Line the bowl of the glass with the **thin-cut peel of ½ lemon**. In a mixing glass, combine **2 oz [60 ml] cognac**; **1 tsp imported orange curaçao***, Grand Marnier, or, for something different, maraschino liqueur; **½ tsp simple syrup** (see Sweetening, page 21); and **1 tsp freshly squeezed lemon juice**** with **cracked ice** and stir well. Strain into the prepared glass. **MAKES 1 DRINK**

* The domestic stuff is too weak, too sweet, and, usually, too artificial to make a satisfying cocktail.
** Most modern recipes call for too much lemon juice and too much liqueur. Unlike modern cocktails, the point here isn't to submerge the flavor of the liquor in some greater whole, but to merely accent it and soften some of its edge.

Clover Club

People rarely make drinks with egg whites at home anymore, but in this case it's worth it—the Clover Club is unusual, tasty, strong, and not at all slimy. You may garnish this drink with a fresh mint leaf, but be warned that turns the Clover Club into a Clover Leaf.

In a cocktail shaker, combine **1 oz [30 ml] London dry gin**, **1 oz [30 ml] dry vermouth**, **1 egg white**, **½ oz [15 ml] freshly squeezed lemon juice**, and **2 tsp raspberry syrup** with **ice** and shake well. Strain into a chilled cocktail glass.
MAKES 1 DRINK

Dark and Stormy

In the mid-nineteenth century, the Royal Navy started issuing ginger beer to its sailors in the hope that some of them would choose it over their daily rum ration. No doubt some did. The sensible ones, however, poured the latter into the former. The key here is nailing the precise ratio between the spice of the ginger beer and the richness of the rum. Use a funky, dark, and potent rum. Depending on the brands of each used, you may want to play around with the proportions. No true Bermudian would put lime juice in his D&S, but in the States that's how it comes (perhaps the Moscow mule has something to do with that). Frankly, we prefer it with the lime—but we're not Bermudian, now, are we? In fact, we've never even been to the "still-vexed Bermoothes," as Shakespeare calls 'em.

Combine **2 oz [60 ml] dark rum***, **3 oz [90 ml] ginger beer****, and **½ oz [15 ml] freshly squeezed lime juice** (optional) in a tall glass full of **ice cubes**. Stir briefly, garnish with **a lime wedge**, and serve. **MAKES 1 DRINK**

* *Bermuda's own Gosling's Black Seal is, of course, the preferred brand, but anything dark and funky will work.*
** *If you can find Barritt's, use that. It's from Bermuda. If you can't find it, anything will work—as long as it's ginger beer and not ginger ale.*

French 75

A Prohibition-era hack on the Tom Collins, wherein the weak, unintoxicating soda water is replaced with Champagne. What could possibly go wrong? (If serving these, make your guests sign a waiver.)

In a cocktail shaker, combine **½ oz [15 ml] freshly squeezed lemon juice** and **1 tsp sugar**, stir briefly, and add **1 ½ oz [45 ml] gin** or VSOP-grade cognac (there are two schools here, both alike in dignity). Shake well and pour into a Collins glass full of **cracked ice**. Top off with **chilled Champagne.** (Note: Some prefer their French 75s served without the ice, in which case you can make them in Champagne flutes.) **MAKES 1 DRINK**

Gin Rickey

Esquire's **official drink** of summer—second only in refreshment to icy mountain spring water drunk straight from the source. Okay, maybe third—see Green Swizzle, page 84.

Put **3 or 4 ice cubes** in a tall glass. Squeeze in the **juice from ½ lime** and drop in the spent lime shell. Add **1 ½ oz [45 ml] gin**. Top off with **chilled club soda** or seltzer water. **MAKES 1 DRINK**

Green Swizzle

In the summer months, we need drinks that aren't just cooling but are *tall* and cooling. The hydrating Mojito. The swamp-cutting gin rickey. The heat-desensitizing julep. Or the most cooling of all: The mighty swizzle.

In a Collins glass, combine **2 oz [60 ml] mellow dry gin** such as Plymouth or Fords, or flavorful white rum such as Banks 5 Island; **1 oz [30 ml] Velvet Falernum**; **½ oz [15 ml] freshly squeezed lime juice**; and **1 barspoon wormwood bitters** or absinthe*. Fill the glass all the way with **finely cracked ice**. Add **chilled seltzer water** to fill. Swizzle until the glass frosts or you tire of swizzling, whichever occurs first. Shake in **6 to 8 dashes Angostura bitters**—enough to cover the top. Garnish with **a mint sprig** and add a straw to serve. **MAKES 1 DRINK**

* If using absinthe, use a non-anisey Czech-style one, such as Mata Hari, rather than a French or domestic one. If you're the maker sort, the bitters are ridiculously easy to concoct. Steep ½ oz [15 g] or so of dried wormwood in 2 cups [480 ml] of J. Wray & Nephew white overproof rum for 2 days, strain through a coffee filter, and bottle.

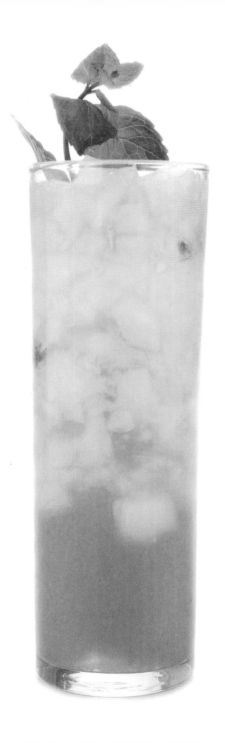

Hot Buttered Rum

This drink probably makes sense only to tenth-generation Yankees from Down East, but when the snow is measured in yardsticks and the mercury is in hibernation it somehow works. Make sure to use the darkest, richest Jamaican or Demerara rum you can get. You may substitute cider for the water and add ½ tsp mixed ground cinnamon and cloves, but that's getting away from the rock-ribbed simplicity of the thing. If you're a real purist, put everything in a mug and then ram a red-hot poker into it until it steams— a most satisfying operation, but not to be considered after round three.

In a mug, dissolve **2 sugar cubes** in a little **hot water**, then add **2 oz [60 ml] dark rum** and **a pat of unsalted butter**. Fill the mug with hot water and stir to melt the butter. Grate a little **fresh nutmeg** on top, if you feel the calling (we generally take ours without). **MAKES 1 DRINK**

Irish Coffee

The Irish coffee needs no persuasion or recommendation to ease its path through the world. One taste of a properly executed example and its existence will always be with you. When you're cold, tired, or a little blue, it will help.

Lightly whip **½ cup [120 ml] organic heavy cream** (you want the kind that's pure cream) by whisking it in a bowl or shaking the bejesus out of it in an empty cocktail shaker. Set aside. Put **1 tsp Demerara** or turbinado sugar in a London dock glass*. Add **3 to 4 oz [90 to 120 ml] hot black coffee** and stir to dissolve the sugar. Add **1½ oz [45 ml] full-bodied Irish whiskey** such as Redbreast, Bushmills, Black Bush, or Powers and stir again. Top with a 1-in [2.5-cm] layer of the whipped cream. Smile.
MAKES 1 DRINK

*The glass every Irish whiskey you've ever had has been served in. With the pedestal.
And the impractically small handle for hands daintier than yours.*

Jack Rose

This drink is based on applejack, and it's rose pink. Play on words. It's smooth and sweetish and deeply deceptive. Sipping it, you can't tell it contains liquor of any kind, let alone applejack.

In a cocktail shaker, combine **2 oz [60 ml] applejack**, **1 oz [30 ml] freshly squeezed lime juice**, and **½ oz [15 ml] grenadine** with **cracked ice** and shake well. Strain into a chilled cocktail glass. **MAKES 1 DRINK**

Mai Tai

~~~~~~

Oh, how the mai tai has suffered. But when the experiment is performed correctly....

In a cocktail shaker, combine **2 oz [60 ml] dark rum**, **½ oz [15 ml] imported orange curaçao**, **1 oz [30 ml] freshly squeezed lime juice**, **½ oz [15 ml] orgeat syrup**, and **1 tsp rock candy syrup** (see Sweeteners, page 21) with **ice** and shake well. Pour, unstrained, into a large Collins glass (or, of course, a tiki mug). Garnish with **a squeezed-out lime half** and **a sprig of fresh mint**. **MAKES 1 DRINK**

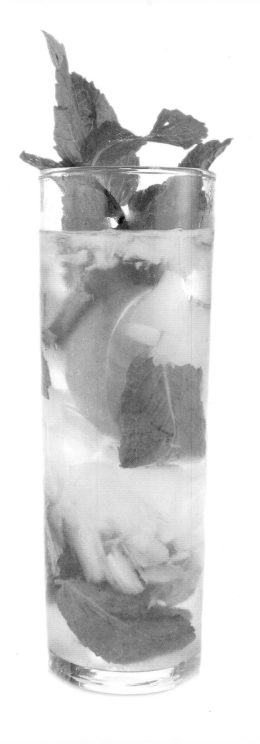

Mojito

In Cuban hands, the Mojito is a clean, simple drink that lets you get a considerable amount of the creature under your belt with almost no pain or fuss. Unfortunately, everyone else in the world seems to be falling over each other in an attempt to complicate the thing. There's no need.

In a smallish Collins glass, stir **½ oz [15 ml] freshly squeezed lime juice** with **½ to 1 tsp superfine sugar***. Add **a few fresh mint leaves** and press them lightly with a muddler. Fill the glass two-thirds full with **cracked ice** and pour in **1 ½ oz [45 ml] flavorful white rum****. Top off with **a splash of chilled club soda** or seltzer water and insert **a sprig of mint**. Serve with a stirring rod. **MAKES 1 DRINK**

* Depending on how sweet you like 'em; we like ours a bit tart.
** Havana Club three-year-old is ideal, especially now that it's legal to hand-import it.

Moscow Mule

Vodka's breakout cocktail—simply because it was marketed aggressively by the first big vodka brand in the United States, Smirnoff. Professional bartenders in the '40s and '50s hated it, but the suckers bit. At least the Moscow mule is easy, smooth, and refreshing. Taken by itself, it does no harm, and compared to so much that has followed, it's practically elegant.

Add **½ oz [15 ml] freshly squeezed lime juice** to a Collins glass (or Moscow mule mug) and drop in one of the spent lime shells. Add **2 or 3 ice cubes**, then pour in **2 oz [60 ml] vodka** and top off with **chilled ginger beer** (not ginger ale, although what the hell). **MAKES 1 DRINK**

The First Silly Vodka Cocktail

The Moscow mule is not, by the way, the first silly vodka drink. That distinction belongs to the Blue Monday, first printed in the English Savoy bar book in 1930. The Blue Monday, which appears to have been quite popular in Europe, mixes vodka with a splash of Cointreau, which is just a superior brand of Triple Sec or white curaçao, and blue food coloring. It's a simple step to premix the curaçao and the dye, yielding blue curaçao—the first truly artificial liqueur (unless there's a strain of cerulean blue oranges out there we don't know about).

PEGU CLUB

Pegu Club

Among all the far-flung outposts of the British Empire, few were flung farther than Rangoon's Pegu Club, right there at the corner of Prome Road and Newlyn Road. Unlike the Muthaiga Country Club and the Ootacamund Club, the Pegu Club managed to insert itself into the annals of mixology with a delightful and refreshing combination of gin (naturally), lime juice, orange curaçao, and a couple of other thises and thats. You can substitute Grand Marnier for orange curaçao.

In a cocktail shaker, combine **2 oz [60 ml] London dry gin**, **¾ oz [22 ml] imported orange curaçao**, **½ oz [15 ml] freshly squeezed lime juice**, **1 dash Angostura bitters**, and **1 dash orange bitters** with **ice** and shake well. Strain into a chilled cocktail glass and garnish with **a lime wheel. MAKES 1 DRINK**

Pisco Sour

The pisco sour is the national drink of Peru and one of the world's great cocktails. The drink came about when some anonymous Johnny Cocktailseed introduced the cocktail shaker and its proper use to Peru. That was some time before 1903, when the drink first appeared in print. In Peru, the preferred style of pisco—the local un-oaked grape brandy—for a sour is *acholado*, a blend of aromatic and neutral-flavored grapes. For a more floral sour, use an "Italia" style.

In a cocktail shaker, combine **2 oz [60 ml] pisco**, **¾ oz [22 ml] freshly squeezed lime juice**, **¾ oz [22 ml] simple syrup** (see Sweetening, page 21), and **1 egg white** with **cracked ice** and shake well. Strain into a large, chilled cocktail glass. Add **3 or 4 drops Angostura bitters** on the foam. **MAKES 1 DRINK**

Ramos Fizz

This isn't a drink to throw together from whatever you've got lying around; every part of the formula is crucial. The egg white gives it body, the cream lends smoothness, and the citrus provides coolth. The sugar tames the citrus, the gin does what gin does, and the seltzer wakes up the whole thing. As for the orange flower water—that's for mystery.

In a cocktail shaker, combine **½ oz [15 ml] freshly squeezed lemon juice**, **½ oz [15 ml] freshly squeezed lime juice**, and **2 tsp superfine sugar**. Stir to dissolve the sugar. Add **1 ½ oz [45 ml] London dry gin** or Plymouth gin (you want a fairly soft gin here), **1 oz [30 ml] heavy cream**, **1 egg white**, and **2 or 3 drops orange flower water***. Fill the shaker with **ice**, shake viciously for at least a minute—preferably two—and strain into a chilled Collins glass that has **1 oz [30 ml] chilled club soda** or seltzer water in it. Top up with additional club soda, if needed. **MAKES 1 DRINK**

Don't bother substituting orange juice or orange liqueur or orange anything else for the orange flower water; it has a fragrance unrelated to that of the fruit. Also, do not use half-and-half in place of the cream. As for the gin, some old recipes call for Old Tom gin. If that's your gin of choice, dial the sugar back a notch or two.

Remsen Cooler

Some say it's a Scotch drink. Others, gin. (Those others are right.) At least everybody agrees on what you do with the booze—put it in a glass with a long lemon peel and add ice and soda water. Or ginger ale. And maybe sugar. And that lemon peel? You can use orange instead. Okay, the Remsen Cooler's got identity issues. Tasty, though, however it presents.

Peel **1 whole lemon** in one long spiral "as you would an apple" (as Cocktail Bill Boothby said, back in 1908)*. Put the peel in a highball glass, add **2 oz [60 ml] gin** and **½ tsp superfine sugar** (to get the Old Tom effect, unless you're using Old Tom), and stir to dissolve the sugar, making sure to mash the lemon peel up against the glass as well. Then throw in **2 or 3 ice cubes** and top off with **chilled club soda** or seltzer water.
MAKES 1 DRINK

* You don't need a fresh peel for each round, thank God; one is good for two or three uses.

Rob Roy

This is simply a Manhattan with Scotch instead of rye (Rob Roy being a Scottish national hero of some sort). Perhaps a little odd, but in the long run quite rewarding.

In a mixing glass, combine **2 oz [60 ml] blended Scotch whisky, 1 oz [30 ml] Italian vermouth**, and **1 dash Angostura bitters** with **cracked ice** and stir well. Strain into a chilled cocktail glass and garnish as you would a Manhattan—with **a cherry** or a swatch of orange peel. **MAKES 1 DRINK**

Rusty Nail

This drink is where swank ingredients (Drambuie ain't cheap) and homey comfort (the liqueur and ice blunt any edge the liquor might have) meet foolproof construction (there's really no way to screw this one up—if it's too sweet, just add more Scotch). The quantities here are a rough ratio. Fifty-fifty is too sweet for us, but some folks swear by it. We suggest you start with 2 oz [60 ml] Scotch and ½ oz [15 ml] Drambuie and work your way up from there (or, of course, stop). There are those who insist on layering the ingredients. Nah.

Combine **2 oz [60 ml] Scotch*** and **½ oz [15 ml] Drambuie** in a double old-fashioned glass, add lots of **ice**, and stir before serving. **MAKES 1 DRINK**

* *Blended Scotch is traditional, but use a good one. Johnnie Walker Black, Dewar's 12. You get the idea.*

A

Drinker's
MANIFESTO

What should a bar be? What should a bartender be?
How long should it take to make a drink?
What makes a good drink, anyway? A few answers,
guidelines, and pronouncements.

①
Drinking is fun.

②
Drinking is everything
you do while drinking,
including talking, going
to the john, and over-
hearing the conversa-
tions of others.

③
Craft cocktails tend
to take a long time to
make. Mixology.

④
At a place that serves
craft cocktails, a drinker
may order a second drink
before he has finished
the first. Logistics.

⑤
Bars are
not temples of
mixology.

⑥
Drinkers aren't
supplicants.

7

Although when the bartender at the temple of mixology puts half your Manhattan in a separate vessel and nestles that vessel in a bowl of crushed ice and places it next to your glass? That's worthy of praise. Very cold cocktails always are.

8

However, sometimes you don't want a craft cocktail, because sometimes it doesn't taste better. Sometimes it's raining and your flight is delayed and you're a couple time zones from home, and you just want the lady wearing the maroon vest behind the bar to pour some gin into a glass with some tonic, and you just want to drink it and smile and think of home.

9

A drinker should be tended to. If a bartender serving a modest crowd does not ask if you want another drink upon your finishing your drink, then that bartender is a bad bartender.

10

It is not known who supplies the restroom graffiti, but their efforts are worthy of appreciation.

11

A bar may not always improve a mood. And it can make it worse.

12

A drink can improve a mood. Because it is made with alcohol, which is a drug.

13

Sometimes a bartender's mustache is just a mustache. Usually not, but sometimes. Depends what kind of bar you're in.

14

You can chuckle at the presence of house-made bitters—we all have. But know this: The house-made bitters are terrific. And they improve a drink.

15

And look, they're not going to the trouble of making bitters because they don't care how your drink tastes.

16

The best bartender conversations do not involve the discussion of spirits.

17

If you get even the slightest feeling that the bartender feels he is doing you a favor by mixing you a drink, you are in the wrong bar.

18

With a few exceptions the best bartender is a smiling bartender. Because drinking is fun.

Sazerac

Sometimes it takes a cold drink to light a fire inside, and few do the job quite so well as New Orleans' storied Sazerac cocktail, a dark, rich, and bracing dram whose powers of warming are high and cooling practically nil. Perverse. But then again, New Orleans is a perverse sort of place.

Chill a small rocks glass by putting it in the freezer. In a mixing glass, muddle **1 sugar cube** with **3 dashes Peychaud's Bitters** (accept no substitute) and a **barspoon of water** until the sugar is dissolved. Fill the glass with **cracked ice**. Add **2 oz [60 ml] straight rye whiskey***. Stir. Retrieve the chilled rocks glass, pour in a **barspoon or so of absinthe**, swirl it around, and pour it out. Strain the contents of the mixing glass into the absinthe-rinsed one and twist **a swatch of thin-cut lemon peel** over the top and drop it in. Smile and serve. **MAKES 1 DRINK**

* In order of desirability: Rittenhouse 100 proof, Wild Turkey (the rye, not the bourbon), Sazerac, or Old Overholt.

Sidecar

The sidecar is one of the great lifesavers in the cocktail family tree. A French creation from around 1918, it was the drink that greeted American travelers with open arms when they arrived in Europe seeking respite from the deprivations of Prohibition—the drink that convinced them that the Fine Art of Mixing Drinks might possibly have a future to match its illustrious past. Made with good, rich cognac, the sidecar is a peerlessly sophisticated cocktail that is also both simple and sneakily potent.

Run **a lemon wedge** around the rim of a chilled cocktail glass, then dip the moist rim in a plate of **sugar** and let dry. In a cocktail shaker, combine **1½ oz [45 ml] VSOP-grade cognac**, **¾ oz [22 ml] Cointreau**, and **½ oz [15 ml] freshly squeezed lemon juice** with lots of **ice** and shake well. Strain into the prepared cocktail glass. **MAKES 1 DRINK**

Singapore Sling

This recipe for the much-disputed classic comes from a 1948 cocktail guide written by one John Kelly, an undoubtedly upstanding citizen who had run a liquor-importing business in Shanghai before the Japanese chased him out. Once back in the States, he claimed that he got his sling recipe directly from the good people at Raffles Hotel in Singapore. We have no reason to doubt him, and with its twin virtues of simplicity and deliciousness, we daresay we believe in him. In later years, the Raffles would drown their sling in a sticky mass of fruit juice, but when Kelly was there, at least, they were holding the line.

In a tall glass, combine **1½ oz [45 ml] London dry gin** (Beefeater or Tanqueray), **1½ oz [45 ml] Cherry Heering**, and **½ oz [15 ml] freshly squeezed lime juice**. Add **ice**, stir, and top off with **1 oz [30 ml] chilled seltzer water**. Float **½ oz [15 ml] Plymouth sloe gin** over the top, garnish with **a lime wheel**, and serve with a straw.
MAKES 1 DRINK

Ti' Punch

Few drinks can hold their own with the old fashioned when it comes to simplicity, tradition, and straightforward deliciousness. This is one of them. Down in Martinique and Guadeloupe, *rhum agricole** country, the ti' punch is the preferred way of absorbing the daily ration of the stuff—ti' being how you say *petit* in the Creole they speak there. But watch out! Any drink that has "little" in its name is like the guy they call "Tiny"—the one standing over by the keg whom you mistook for a piece of earthmoving equipment.

Cut a 1-in (2.5-cm) disk off the side of **a lime**, getting a small amount of the flesh. In an old-fashioned glass, combine **2 oz [60 ml]** *rhum agricole*, a good squeeze of the lime disk (squeeze it peel-side down, then drop it into the glass), and anywhere from **1 tsp to 1 Tbsp cane syrup****, depending on how sweet you like your drinks. Stir until the syrup is dissolved. Add **1 or 2 ice cubes**, stir again, and drink. (To make ti' punches for a crowd, it's best to do as the Martiniquais do and "let each prepare his own death," as they say. Simply cut a bunch of lime disks, put them in a bowl, and arrange on a tray along with a bottle of *rhum agricole*, one of cane syrup, and a bucket of ice. Add the appropriate glassware and a barspoon or two and you're ready for company.) **MAKES 1 DRINK**

* Rhum agricole—literally, "agricultural rum"—is distilled not from molasses, as most rums are, but rather from fresh sugarcane juice. Dry and grassy, it has a funky edge that is impossible to otherwise obtain. In Martinique, the white version, which usually clocks in at 50 percent alcohol, is traditional for this drink, but an aged one works fine as well. If you can find Neisson, J.M., or La Favorite, those are excellent brands, but Clément makes a fine 50-percenter as well, and it's more widely available.
** Cane syrup, familiar to residents of the Caribbean or Deep South, can be hard to find elsewhere; about the only thing we can suggest as a substitute is boiling up ½ cup [120 ml] water with 1 cup [200 g] unrefined sugar. Let it cool, bottle it, and store it in the refrigerator.

Tom and Jerry

The Tom and Jerry was a holiday favorite for a century. The '60s, with its thirst for novelty and mania for convenience, killed it off, but you can still find the mugs—little white ceramic things with "Tom & Jerry" printed in gold—in back-country thrift shops (or on eBay, of course). This one may require practice and a certain amount of fiddling, but it's well worth the effort.

Separate **12 eggs**. In a bowl, beat the egg whites until they form a stiff froth. In another bowl, beat the yolks with **1 cup [200 g] sugar** "until they are as thin as water," as the professor advises, while gradually adding **4 oz [120 ml] brandy** (spiceaholics will also add a pinch each of ground allspice, cinnamon, and cloves). Fold the whites into the yolk mixture. When ready to serve, give the base another stir, then spoon 1 Tbsp of this batter into a small mug or tumbler. Add **1 oz [30 ml] brandy** (although some diehard Dixiecrats prefer bourbon) and **1 oz [30 ml] Jamaican rum**, stirring constantly to avoid curdling. Fill to the top with **hot milk*** and stir until you get foam. Grate a little **fresh nutmeg** on top. **MAKES 1 DRINK**

* Some people find the milk too rich and filling, so they use half hot milk, half boiling water.

VESPER

Vesper

The Vesper martini, as Bond christened his drink in *Casino Royale*, should be a Sean Connery among cocktails: smooth and debonair, yet not without a nasty kick. But as it's usually made, it isn't. Let's fix that. Shaking it, as 007 requests, gives it a thin and unsatisfying texture. If you stir it instead, it'll be as silky as Pussy Galore's intimate apparel. (We've included a couple of other little tweaks as well.)

In a mixing glass, combine **3 oz [90 ml] Tanqueray gin**, **1 oz [30 ml] 100-proof Stolichnaya vodka**, and **½ oz [15 ml] Cocchi Americano** or ½ oz Lillet* plus **1 barspoon artisanal tonic water** with plenty of **cracked ice** and stir well (if you must shake, shake—but who are you going to trust, a shifty government employee or ten generations of American bartenders?). Strain into a chilled cocktail glass and twist **a large swatch of thin-cut lemon peel** over the top. Drink up. Shoot somebody evil. **MAKES 1 DRINK**

* The Lillet that Fleming called for apparently had a higher quinine content than the current version; the Cocchi has that bitter edge.

Vieux Carre

Walter Bergeron held down the bar at New Orleans' Monteleone Hotel in the last years before Prohibition. After Repeal, the hotel brought him back. When he returned, it was with a new drink, one that has since become a New Orleans classic.

In a mixing glass, stir **1 oz [30 ml] VSOP-grade cognac**, **1 oz [30 ml] rye whiskey**, **1 oz [30 ml] sweet vermouth**, **1 barspoon Bénédictine**, **1 dash Angostura bitters**, and **1 dash Peychaud's Bitters** with **cracked ice** and strain into a chilled cocktail glass. Twist **a swatch of thin-cut lemon peel** over the top and drop it in. **MAKES 1 DRINK**

Ward Eight Cooler

This Boston classic is normally a cocktail—straight up, no soda—but it makes an excellent cooler.

In a cocktail shaker, combine **2 oz [60 ml] straight rye whiskey**, **¾ oz [22 ml] freshly squeezed orange juice**, **½ oz [15 ml] freshly squeezed lemon juice**, and a generous **1 tsp grenadine** with plenty of **cracked ice** and shake well. Pour unstrained, ice and all, into a sturdy glass and top off with **chilled club soda. MAKES 1 DRINK**

White Russian

Like its cousin the Brandy Alexander, the White Russian so effectively lubricates the hefty dose of alcohol it contains that it goes down the hatch with no resistance whatsoever. Some folks build this one on the rocks, floating the cream on top.

In a cocktail shaker, combine **1 ½ oz [45 ml] vodka**, **¾ oz [22 ml] Kahlúa**, and **¾ oz [22 ml] heavy cream** with **ice** and shake well. Strain into a chilled old-fashioned glass (it'll look less wicked than in a martini glass; that's important). **MAKES 1 DRINK**

How to
DRINK WITH YOUR WIFE

~~~~~~

BY BARRY SONNENFELD

On a typical evening, depending on the time of year, Sweetie (the wife) and I will have some sort of drink. Around four o'clock, I'll join her in the den with a reminder that in one hour I will be asking her what she'll want to drink that night, and that she should start thinking about it now. A half hour later, I'll remind her again, and at five, I'll ask her what she's decided. Without fail, she'll need another half hour to think about it. At some point, just to accelerate her thought process, I'll announce my selection for the evening, which often changes based on her eventual choice.

For us, "martini" is a loose term for me brutally shaking many ounces of alcohol in a shaker. (Oxo makes an excellent one that is like a thermos, double-lined so you can shake longer without giving your hands freezer burn.) What we're really looking for is cold booze in a beautiful glass. It might be vodka or tequila—*añejo* or silver. In the winter, I might have a dry Rob Roy (Scotch, dry vermouth, and a twist). Sweetie, on the other hand, has taken a liking to Hendrick's-gin martinis, served with a cucumber spear. I tried to steer her away from gin, fearing that it makes for an angry drunk, but so far that hasn't happened. She's delightful. (So is our nine-year-old Rhodesian ridgeback. He's developed a Pavlovian response to cocktail hour. As soon as he hears me scooping manly amounts of ice into our glasses to chill, he stands up and heads for our bar to eat ice cubes. I've convinced him they're a treat.)

The endless frustration comes when we decide to drink Champagne. We have many styles of Champagne flutes, but no matter which one I pick, it isn't the style Sweetie wants that night. Lately I've taken to bringing her three distinct choices from the bar. Even then, none will satisfy her. I've begun to realize that her daily choice of booze is more an unconscious reflection of what kind of glass she wants to hold than of the liquor she wants to drink. My choice is a reflection of what's important to me, so I'll have what she's having.

Zombie

By the time tiki culture hit its stride in the '50s, the zombie, with all its evil, no-more-than-two-to-a-customer charm, was ubiquitous. Unfortunately, that didn't mean it was any good. In fact, it's not. But no matter—sometimes the urge will strike anyway. (The juice in the recipe is what mixologist David Embury calls the "mystery ingredient"; it can be pineapple juice, passion fruit nectar, coconut milk, or apricot or cherry brandy—just about anything this side of Romilar.)

In a cocktail shaker, combine **1½ oz [45 ml] golden rum**, **1 oz [30 ml] dark rum**, **½ oz [15 ml] white rum**, **1 oz [30 ml] freshly squeezed lime juice**, **1 tsp pineapple juice**, **1 tsp papaya juice**, and **1 tsp superfine sugar** with a lot of **ice** and shake well. Strain into a 14-oz [420-ml] glass three-fourths full of cracked ice. Float **½ oz [15 ml] 151-proof rum** on top by pouring it into a spoon and gently dipping it under the surface of the drink. Then, if the spirit moves you, take a match to this mixture; it will burn. Garnish with **a sprig of fresh mint** (either straight or dipped in lime juice and then superfine sugar) and/or fruit. (A particularly fetching touch: On a toothpick, impale a lemon slice or pineapple cube between two maraschino cherries and set this fruit kabob atop the drink.) Supply a straw and, after two of these, a hammock. After three—a stretcher. **MAKES 1 DRINK**

THE THIRD ROUND

The Odd, Inventive, or Surprisingly Good

Ace of Clubs

The original recipe for this 1930s Bermudian drink calls for a full 1 oz [30 ml] crème de cacao. No. The careful dripping of four drops (not dashes) of Angostura bitters on top of the drink, while not essential, will add a special something not to be sneezed at. Also, try to use Barbados rum, if you have it. Smooth, seductive, and not too sweet.

In a cocktail shaker, combine **2 oz [60 ml] golden rum**, **½ oz [15 ml] white crème de cacao**, **½ oz [15 ml] freshly squeezed lime juice**, and **½ tsp simple syrup** (see Sweetening, page 21) with **ice** and shake well. Strain into a chilled cocktail glass. **MAKES 1 DRINK**

Alley Cat

The caraway flavor of the kümmel* combines with the rye to make this drink spicy, even frisky.

In a mixing glass, combine **2 oz [60 ml] Sazerac rye, 1 oz [30 ml] Sandeman Founders Reserve port, 1 tsp Helbing kümmel**, and **2 dashes Angostura bitters** with **cracked ice** and stir well. Strain into a chilled cocktail glass. **MAKES 1 DRINK**

A characteristic cordial of Prussia and its neighbors, kümmel is a caraway-and-cumin-flavored liqueur, and on the dry side.

Americano

The Americano is a fine alternative to a glass of beer on a hot day—slightly bitter, slightly sweet, it's tall and refreshing and very, very easy to drink.

In a tall glass, combine **1 ½ oz [45 ml] sweet red vermouth** and **1 ½ oz [45 ml] Campari** and stir. Add **2 or 3 ice cubes** and top off with **chilled seltzer water**. Garnish with **half an orange wheel. MAKES 1 DRINK**

Armagnac Cocktail

The Armagnac version of the old Netherland cocktail, a New York specialty dating back at least to 1914, is simple to make, strong—very strong—and mellow, and if you use a good curaçao, not too sweet.

In a cocktail shaker, combine **2 oz [60 ml] VSOP-grade Armagnac** or Napoleon Armagnac, **1 oz [30 ml] imported orange curaçao** or Grand Marnier, and **2 dashes Regans' Orange Bitters No. 6** with lots of **ice** and shake viciously. Strain into a chilled cocktail glass. **MAKES 1 DRINK**

BATISTE

Batiste

The Batiste, collected by *Esquire* back in the 1930s, is a friendly little cocktail and easy on the eye. Add the juice of ½ lime and a twist of lemon peel and you have a Prince George.

In a cocktail shaker, combine **2 oz [60 ml] white rum** and **1 oz [30 ml] Grand Marnier** with plenty of **ice** and shake energetically. Strain into a chilled cocktail glass. **MAKES 1 DRINK**

The Bone

Whiskey and Tabasco. Which says it all. (And it also tastes good.)

In a cocktail shaker, combine **2 oz [60 ml] 101-proof Wild Turkey rye** or bourbon, **1 tsp freshly squeezed lime juice**, **1 tsp simple syrup** (see Sweetening, page 21), and **3 dashes Tabasco sauce** with **ice** and shake well. Strain into a chilled tall shot glass. **MAKES 1 DRINK**

Borden Chase

A particularly tasty 1930s variation on the Rob Roy. Borden Chase—real name, Frank Fowler—wrote the screenplay for *Red River*. Cheers, Borden!

In a mixing glass, combine **2 ¼ oz [68 ml] blended Scotch whisky***, **¾ oz [22 ml] Italian vermouth**, **½ tsp Pernod****, and **2 dashes orange bitters** with **cracked ice** and stir well. Strain into a chilled cocktail glass. **MAKES 1 DRINK**

* Some suggestions: Pinch, Johnnie Walker Black, and White Horse.
** You can use another pastis, such as Ricard, Herbsaint, Absente, or Pastis Henri Bardouin.

Brain Duster

Back around 1890, the Broadway swells came up with a new name for the kind of drink that, when thrown down the hatch, knocked your head back, kicked you in the ass, and made you walk around in a little circle emitting sounds not recognizable as speech: a "brain duster." Here's one of their versions; if you want a more modern version, try 1½ oz [45 ml] Ardbeg, Laphroaig, or other heavily peated Scotch whisky, preferably cask strength, and ½ oz [15 ml] Fernet Branca shaken with ice and strained into a tall shot glass.

In a mixing glass, combine **1 oz [30 ml] rye whiskey***, **1 oz [30 ml] absinthe**, **1 oz [30 ml] Italian vermouth**, and **1 dash Angostura bitters** with **cracked ice** and stir well. Strain into a chilled cocktail glass. **MAKES 1 DRINK**

* Use something around 100 proof for maximum efficacy. You can also use bourbon.

BROWN DERBY

Brown Derby

New England's answer to the daiquiri. It might not be tropical, but it sure is tasty.

In a cocktail shaker, combine **2 oz [60 ml] dark rum***, **1 oz [30 ml] freshly squeezed lime juice**, and **1 tsp maple sugar**** with **ice** and shake well. Strain into a chilled cocktail glass. **MAKES 1 DRINK**

* One of the new, local New England rums would be appropriate here, such as Old Ipswich. Use an aged one. Failing that, use a good, rich Jamaican or Guyanese rum.
** Maple syrup is a lot cheaper and works just as well.

Burnt Fuselage

A simple one from 1920s Paris. Exceptionally tasty, if somewhat grim—the drink was created by Chuck Kerwood, a Philadelphian who served in the French air force in World War I and saw a lot of planes go down in flames.

In a mixing glass, combine **1 oz [30 ml] VSOP-grade cognac**, **1 oz [30 ml] Grand Marnier**, and **1 oz [30 ml] dry (white) French vermouth** with **cracked ice** and stir well. Strain into a chilled cocktail glass. Twist **a swatch of thin-cut lemon peel** over the top and drop it in.
MAKES 1 DRINK

Café Cocktail

We were skeptical when we came across this formula in a list of drinks that *Esquire* test-drove just before World War II. We generally like a little more octane; and besides, the recipe makes it sound way too sweet. We were wrong.

In a mixing glass, combine **1 oz [30 ml] cognac, 1 oz [30 ml] crème de cacao, 2 oz [60 ml] coffee**, and **1 tsp superfine sugar** with **cracked ice** and stir well. Strain into a chilled cocktail glass and garnish with **a twist of lemon peel. MAKES 1 DRINK**

Cape Codder

Admittedly, there's not much to the ol' Cape Codder. Made right, though, it's pleasant and refreshing and just a little bit surprising.

Pour **2 oz [60 ml] vodka** or—and here's what will make it surprising—good, flavorful white rum into a Collins glass. Add **2 to 3 oz [60 to 90 ml] cranberry juice cocktail**, the **juice of ½ lime** (some leave this out), and a couple of **ice cubes**. Stir. Top off with **chilled club soda** or seltzer water (some leave this out, too, doubling the cranberry; we don't). Garnish, if you wish, with **a lime wheel** and/or a sprig of mint.
MAKES 1 DRINK

CHICAGO FIZZ

Chicago Fizz

A genteel drink from Chicago—obviously the part where Frank Lloyd Wright built houses, not the part where roughnecks butchered pigs and put them in cans. For an Elks' Club Fizz, use rye whiskey instead of rum and garnish with a bit of pineapple.

In a cocktail shaker, combine **1 oz [30 ml] dark rum**, **1 oz [30 ml] ruby port**, **½ oz [15 ml] freshly squeezed lemon juice**, **½ tsp superfine sugar**, and **½ egg white*** with **ice** and shake well. Strain into a chilled small Collins glass and fizz with **seltzer water** to 1 in [2.5 cm] or so from the top**. **MAKES 1 DRINK**

* You can leave out the egg white, if you like, without affecting the taste. But it does add a sturdy body to the drink, along with a nice opacity. Plus, there's the protein.
** If you don't have a soda siphon (an entirely pardonable oversight), give the seltzer bottle a careful little shake before pouring it in. You want bubbles.

Close Call

This one, an example of what happens when you use your drink patterns (here, it's the Manhattan), almost sucks—but then doesn't, at all. Hence the name.

In a mixing glass, combine **2 oz [60 ml] Siembra Azul tequila**, **1 oz [30 ml] Lustau Don Nuño sherry**, **1 tsp Cherry Heering**, and **2 dashes Angostura bitters** with **cracked ice** and stir well. Strain into a chilled cocktail glass. **MAKES 1 DRINK**

Florida

Pleasantly understated, dry, strong, and simple to construct. In other words, it's about as relevant to the Florida of today as Babylonian spelt beer is.

In a cocktail shaker, combine **1 ½ oz [45 ml] dark rum, ¾ oz [22 ml] cognac, 1 ½ oz [45 ml] freshly squeezed grapefruit juice**, and **1 ½ oz [45 ml] freshly squeezed orange juice** with **ice** and shake well. Strain into a Collins glass filled with cracked ice. Garnish with **an orange wheel** and paper umbrella. What the hell. You can't fight progress. **MAKES 1 DRINK**

Florodora

Created back in 1901 for a chorus girl, this one's fragrant, pleasing, and—over the long haul—lethal. For a Florodora Imperial Style, replace the gin with cognac. It's more expensive that way. Chorus girls like that, or so they say.

In a cocktail shaker, combine **2 oz [60 ml] London dry gin**, **½ oz [15 ml] freshly squeezed lime juice**, and **1 tsp raspberry syrup** with **4 or 5 ice cubes** and shake well. Pour, unstrained, into a Collins glass and top off with **chilled ginger ale**.
MAKES 1 DRINK

Glasgow

In the high school of hooch, the Glasgow is the weird kid with artistic tendencies.

In a mixing glass, combine **2 oz [60 ml] blended Scotch whisky, 1 oz [30 ml] French vermouth, 1 tsp absinthe*,** and **a dash Peychaud's Bitters**** with **cracked ice** and stir well. Strain into a chilled cocktail glass. Garnish with . . . a twist? A twig? The head of a Barbie doll? **MAKES 1 DRINK**

* You can always use a substitute—Pernod, Ricard, Herbsaint, like that. In fact, we recommend it. You could also try Chartreuse, Bénédictine, NyQuil, Mrs. Butterworth's . . .
** If you're gonna put bitters in your Scotch, master mixologist David Embury established that these are the ones to use.

Gypsy

Here's one from the hand-cranked era of vodka drinks—the years between the repeal of Prohibition in 1933 and World War II. You can apply this treatment to any of the herbal liqueurs, as long as you've got a good stock of vaguely Eastern European names to attach to the results.

In a mixing glass, combine **2 oz [60 ml] Russian vodka, 1 oz [30 ml] Bénédictine,** and **a dash Angostura bitters** with **cracked ice** and stir well. Strain into a chilled cocktail glass and drop in **a twist of lemon peel. MAKES 1 DRINK**

HONEY BEE

Honey Bee

Otherwise known as the Bee's Knees, the Honeysuckle, and the Airmail (when it's topped off with Champagne, anyway), this little charmer is as agreeable as a drink can get.

Combine **1 ½ tsp honey*** and **1 ½ tsp warm water** in a cocktail shaker and stir until the honey is thoroughly dissolved. Add **2 oz [60 ml] white rum**** and **½ oz [15 ml] freshly squeezed lemon juice**, then shake viciously with **cracked ice** and strain into a chilled cocktail glass. **MAKES 1 DRINK**

* If this is too dry, or if you're feeling charitable, go ahead and add a little more honey.
** According to David Embury, the white rum makes it a Honeysuckle; a Honey Bee requires dark, Jamaican-style rum. Our 1949 Esquire's Handbook for Hosts disagrees. In any case, for God's sake, use something with flavor.

The Ideal Cocktail

From a 1935 souvenir booklet from Havana's La Florida (yeah, Hemingway drank these).

In a cocktail shaker, combine **1 oz [30 ml] sweet vermouth**, **1 oz [30 ml] dry vermouth**, **1 oz [30 ml] dry gin**, **¾ oz [22 ml] freshly squeezed grapefruit juice**, and **1 tsp maraschino liqueur** with **ice** and shake well. Strain into a chilled cocktail glass. **MAKES 1 DRINK**

Drinking with

THE DON

~~~~~~~~~~

BY TOM JUNOD

There was a seat at the bar. The restaurant, on Ninth Avenue in Midtown, was crowded, but at the bar a stool stood like an empty island in a sea of men who were all standing and talking to one another. They were all elaborately dressed, even bejeweled, in sharp suits and two-tone shirts and cuff links; and as soon as I saw them, I asked the restaurant's hostess two questions. One, if I could eat at the restaurant dressed as I was, in jeans and a T-shirt. And two, if I could just go to the bar and take the empty seat.

"Well, you can," she said, "as soon as those men leave." She was very young and chirpy and spoke to me with a mixture of enthusiasm and pity that made me feel as though I had asked my question in broken English. "But their table is ready, so they should be leaving soon."

I waited by the door and looked at the men. There were eight of them. One was about six-foot-seven-inches tall, and he was the only one without a tie. One was about a foot shorter, and all the men gathered around him. He was wearing a suit with a black-and-white pin-dot pattern and a blue shirt with a white spread collar. He had a dark tan; his hair was dyed coal-black and his teeth were bleached so white they flashed

almost blue. He and all the rest of the men did not look so different from the men I'd grown up with, and I decided that they were either salesmen or mobsters.

After about fifteen minutes, the hostess said, "I'd go up and ask them if you could sit down at the bar if I wasn't so scared of them."

"Oh, that's probably because you don't know them," I said.

"No," she said. "That's because I do know them." She sidled up closer to me and whispered, "They're members of the Mafia." Then she took a step back, and her childish face set itself with a pout of sudden resolve. "But you know what? I have cojones, and you've been waiting long enough. I'm going to ask if you can sit down with them."

"You don't have to have cojones on my account," I said, but she was already on her way to talk to the little tanned man. Still smiling, she said something to him, and he studied me through the crowd. Then she waved me over.

I walked to the empty seat without looking at the men. I ordered immediately from a bartender named Victor, and drank an Italian white wine. After about five minutes, I felt a tap on my shoulder.

"What did you order?" asked the man in the black-and-white suit. Up close, his teeth were even brighter and his hair even darker than they had appeared from a distance.

But he looked much older.

"The bucatini," I said.

"With the octopus?" he asked.

I told him yes, and he said, "That's what I order. Did you order it al dente?"

"With all due respect," I said, "the chef is famous. I wouldn't insult him by telling him how to cook."

He thought about this for a second, and then he nodded. "You're right," he said. "They do it pretty good here. You just have to watch out for other places. You never want your bucatini soft."

I went back to drinking my wine and trying to sit as inconspicuously as possible, though I had already been discovered. Victor delivered my first course—raw fish, Italian style—and there was another tap on my shoulder.

"Where are you from?" the man with the bright teeth asked.

"Well, I'm originally from New York, but I live in Georgia."

He tapped himself on the chest. "Me?" he said. "New York. New York. And New York."

My plate of bucatini came out, and I started eating it. A tap on my shoulder, and I turned around. "Can I buy you a martini?" he said. "I consider myself an expert in the martini."

Now, I hate martinis, and never drink them. "Absolutely," I said.

"Victor," he said, and then gestured toward his own drink and then to me. "Like this."

Victor began making the martini under steady scrutiny. The man with the bright teeth began shaking his head, and then said, with sudden vehemence, "Victor, shake the fuck out of it."

Victor began shaking the cocktail extravagantly over his shoulder, like someone who'd been ordered to dance in a movie Western. There was a martini glass set before me, with particles of ice sliding down the sides. Victor poured the martini from the shaker, and it was still slightly effervescent.

"What do you think?" the man with the bright teeth said.

"It's the best martini I've ever had," I said with perfect honesty.

He nodded. "That's because he shook the fuck out of it," he said. Then he signaled to his associates, and they all, at once, repaired to a corner table in the restaurant. I thought of buying him—them—a bottle of wine, but decided that I would risk insulting him, and never came up with an answer to his generosity. I drank my martini down, and when Victor walked away for a moment while settling the bill, I took a look at the cash register and saw the name "Marino, Dan."

The next day, I looked him up on Google and saw that Daniel Marino, seventy-one years old, was one of three bosses in the Gambino crime family. A few months later, I saw that he had pleaded guilty to a charge of conspiracy and been sentenced to serve five years in jail for approving the killing of an informant, who was also his nephew. He is in a prison hospital now, for ailments undisclosed, and whenever I think of him I think of two things.

One, I wonder if he's allowed to blacken his hair in prison and what he looks like white-haired and pale.

And two, I still owe the man a drink.

Junior

The history of the Junior is not only unclear, it's completely unknown. As far as we can tell, its first appearance in print is in the pages of *Esquire*, back in 1937, where it is offered without explanation. No matter. It's a thoroughly sound affair—spicy, rich, and yet cooling.

In a cocktail shaker, combine **2 oz [60 ml] rye whiskey**, **½ oz [15 ml] Bénédictine**, **½ oz [15 ml] freshly squeezed lime juice**, and **a dash of bitters** with **ice** and shake well. Strain into a chilled cocktail glass. **MAKES 1 DRINK**

Knickerbocker

The Knickerbocker, one of the oldest American drinks (circa 1845), is just a little too lush to appeal to the drinker with Puritan tendencies, but it is a suave, delightful little drink for everyone else.

In a cocktail shaker, combine **2 ½ oz [80 ml] golden rum*, ½ tsp imported orange curaçao, 1 ½ tsp raspberry syrup****, and **½ oz [15 ml] freshly squeezed lime juice** with **cracked ice** and shake well. Place one of your spent lime shells in a double old-fashioned glass or small highball glass. (This is the earliest drink on record for which you do this.) Pour the drink in, ice and all***, and garnish with **a few berries** in season: raspberries, blackberries, blueberries—pretty much anything this side of Crunch Berries. Serve with a straw and a little spoon for the berries. **MAKES 1 DRINK**

* Originally, this called for "Santa Cruz" rum, from St. Croix in the Virgin Islands. This still works wonderfully well, but any medium-bodied golden rum will do fine, be it from Barbados, Puerto Rico, Trinidad, or wherever.
** If you can't find this, you can always use Chambord liqueur.
*** If you're making more than one drink at the same time, it's easier to strain the mixture into the glasses first and then add the ice.

Mackinnon

The Drambuie's Scotch base contributes just enough of its smokiness to keep things interesting, while its honey-sweetness is beautifully balanced by the citrus juice and drawn out by the soda. And the rum? Not sure, but the drink isn't nearly as good without it.

In a cocktail shaker, combine **2 oz [60 ml] Drambuie**, ½ oz [15 ml] white rum, ½ oz [15 ml] freshly squeezed lime juice, and ½ oz [15 ml] freshly squeezed lemon juice with **ice** and shake well. Strain into a Collins glass with **2 or 3 ice cubes** in it and top with **chilled club soda** or seltzer water. **MAKES 1 DRINK**

Metropole

There were a lot of Metropole hotels in this country, back when we looked to France for advice on style and design. This comes from the New York one. It's a variation on the Manhattan, sure, but it's an old one—it dates back to around 1884—and, if you spend a little extra on the brandy, a good one.

In a mixing glass, combine **1½ oz [45 ml] VSOP-grade cognac** or Armagnac, **1½ oz [45 ml] dry vermouth**, **2 dashes bitters**, and **cracked ice** and stir well. Strain into a chilled cocktail glass and garnish with **a maraschino cherry. MAKES 1 DRINK**

Montalban

Absolutely seamless. Balanced and delicious.

In a mixing glass, combine **2 oz [60 ml] Mount Gay Eclipse rum, 1 oz [30 ml] Lustau Don Nuño sherry, 1 tsp Cherry Heering, 2 dashes Angostura bitters,** and **cracked ice** and stir well. Strain into a chilled cocktail glass. **MAKES 1 DRINK**

Morning Mist

A smoky cocktail. Not from smoky Scotch, but from smoke.

Put **2 tsp hot water** in a cocktail shaker, add **1 tsp honey,** and stir until the honey is dissolved. Add **1 ½ oz [45 ml] vodka, 1 tsp Bénédictine,** and **½ oz [15 ml] freshly squeezed lemon juice.** Fill the shaker with **ice** and set aside. Stick a straight pin through a 4-in [10-cm] square of corrugated cardboard, impaling a couple of wood chips on the tip, and set the cardboard on a reasonably flameproof surface. Light the wood chips, invert a glass over them, and let the smoke build inside. (Use a Champagne flute or a brandy snifter—something with a stem and a bowl, so the smoke collects tightly.) Now shake the drink thoroughly, flip the glass over, keeping it covered with the cardboard until the last second, and strain the drink into it, using a funnel to get the liquid straight to the bottom. Serve immediately while the layer of smoke still covers the liquid. **MAKES 1 DRINK**

Negrande

A fighty Negroni.

In a mixing glass, combine **1 oz [30 ml] high-proof gin***, **1 oz [30 ml] Gran Classico Bitter**, and **1 oz [30 ml] Dolin blanc vermouth** or Martini & Rossi Bianco sweet white vermouth with **cracked ice** and stir well. Strain into a chilled cocktail coupe. Twist **a swatch of thin-cut orange peel** over the top and drop it in. **MAKES 1 DRINK**

* Such as Old Raj, Hayman's Royal Dock, or Perry's Tot.

The Original Gin Cocktail

Surprisingly, Dutch genever, gin's malty, whiskey-like progenitor, was far more popular than English gins in America from the days of the Founding Fathers until the rise of the martini at the very end of the nineteenth century; when we said "gin," we meant "genever." One of these and you'll see why.

Put **1 cube Demerara sugar** in an old-fashioned glass. Add **½ oz [15 ml] water** and **4 or 5 dashes Fee Brothers whiskey barrel–aged bitters** or the Bitter Truth Old Time Aromatic Bitters. Muddle until the sugar is mostly dissolved. Add **2 oz [60 ml] Bols Genever** or other rich Dutch genever (or genever-style gin from elsewhere). Add **2 cracked ice cubes plus 2 whole cubes.** Stir. Twist **a swatch of thin-cut lemon peel** over the top and drop it in. **MAKES 1 DRINK**

POET'S DREAM

Poet's Dream

There's only one plausible candidate: Wallace Stevens. Not because he's into "behold[ing] the junipers shagged with ice." But because he was a lawyer and a Connecticut insurance executive, two things that in no way contraindicate a dry martini with a splash of Bénédictine—indeed, they practically require it.

In a mixing glass, combine **2 oz [60 ml] London dry gin**, **1 oz [30 ml] French vermouth**, **½ tsp Bénédictine**, and **2 dashes orange bitters** with **cracked ice** and stir well. Strain into a chilled cocktail glass and garnish with **a twist of lemon peel**. **MAKES 1 DRINK**

Rum and Coconut Water

The tropical drink that people in the Caribbean actually drink.

Combine **2 oz [60 ml] golden rum*** and **2 to 4 oz [60 to 120 ml] fresh coconut water**** in a Collins glass, then add **2 or 3 ice cubes**, stir, and serve forth. **MAKES 1 DRINK**

* Our favorite here: one of the aged rums Angostura makes in Trinidad.
** Fresh is best, but the packaged stuff works fine, as long as it's 100 percent coconut water.

Rum Old Fashioned

The result of "rumstitution," which can be applied to so many of the drinks in this book.

Put **1 sugar cube** in an old-fashioned glass. Add **1 tsp water** and **3 dashes Angostura bitters**. Muddle until the sugar is dissolved. Add **2 oz [60 ml] El Dorado 5-year-old rum**. Add **2 cracked ice cubes plus 2 whole cubes**. Stir well. Twist **a thin-cut swatch of orange peel** over the top and drop it in. **MAKES 1 DRINK**

San Martin

What the gents were drinking in Argentina and Uruguay at the turn of the last century. ¡Salud!

In a mixing glass, combine **1½ oz [45 ml] dry gin**, **1½ oz [45 ml] Italian vermouth**, and **1 tsp yellow Chartreuse*** with **cracked ice** and stir well. Strain into a chilled cocktail glass and garnish with **a twist of lemon peel. MAKES 1 DRINK**

* Robert of the Embassy Club calls for the 80-proof yellow kind, while Craddock of the Savoy calls for the 110-proof green. Robert is right. The yellow is mellow, and the drink is less frightful and more delightful. (Besides, between the vermouth and the gin, you've got enough botanicals to go around.)

SAN MARTIN

Sgroppino

In Italy, they have the *sgroppino*, which means, roughly, "little un-knotter." Something to cut a meal.

In a blender, combine **1 oz [30 ml] vodka, 1½ oz [45 ml] lemon sorbet**, and **2 oz [60 ml] finely crushed ice** and blend on high for 20 seconds. Pour into a Champagne flute and top with **Prosecco. MAKES 1 DRINK**

Sherry Cobbler

A universal favorite of the American drinker from 1840 to 1920, and a fine substitute for air-conditioning.

In a cocktail shaker, combine **3 oz [90 ml] oloroso sherry**, **½ oz [15 ml] simple syrup** (see Sweetening, page 21), and **half an orange wheel**. Add **ice**, shake brutally, and strain into a tall glass filled with cracked ice. Garnish with the other half of the orange wheel and **a few berries** in season. **MAKES 1 DRINK**

Sloe Gin Fizz

This old standby—once a morning drink—is one of mixology's more inexpressive products, a simple, mildly (thank God) fruity cooler without much to recommend it besides bland good looks and delicate flavor.

In a cocktail shaker, combine **2 oz [60 ml] imported sloe gin, ½ oz [15 ml] freshly squeezed lemon juice**, and **1 tsp superfine sugar** with **ice** and shake well. Strain into a small, chilled Collins glass and, using a soda siphon, fizz in **chilled club soda** or seltzer water up to 1 in [2.5 cm] or so from the top—or splash the club soda or seltzer in rather carelessly, so that it foams. **MAKES 1 DRINK**

THE NIGHTCAP

BY DAVID WONDRICH

We're not advocating having a big hooker of Scotch before turning in or drinking until you pass out. Managed properly, a nightcap is less about the alcohol than it is about the ritual, about having something rich and soothing to sip while you shrug off the weight of the day. An adult bedtime story. What you want is just a finger of booze or a little more than that of port or other fortified wine, no more. Not enough to mess up your sleep beyond an extra toss or turn or two. If you've been out drinking, you don't need that nightcap—indeed, it would be a bad idea all around. If you're already sleepy, you can skip it. It's not an every-night thing. But when conditions are right, there's nothing more pleasant.

Not every spirit works well as a nightcap. Cordials and liqueurs might be traditional, but their heavy sweetness works better earlier in the evening. (That said, a nip of green Chartreuse makes a good occasional nightcap—just a nip, though; it's 110 proof.) Bourbons and ryes, while wonderful, tend to be mood-breakingly tangy, as does tequila, even when well aged. Vodka lacks comfort; gin—just no. Scotch can be perfect if it's one of the expressions low on the peat, smoke, and sherry-cask tarryness and high on the sweet barley notes and mellowness. Nor do we want super-high-end luxury spirits. The focus of the nightcap isn't on the spirit; it's on the ritual. And we'd rather save those rare drams for when we can concentrate on them fully. You may feel differently about these choices, of course; it's your glass and you know best what you want inside it. We do, however, have a few suggestions.

Most fortified wines—ports, sherries, Madeiras, and such—are too sweet for nightcap work, with the exception of a fino sherry, which is far too dry. Some, however, are perfect. We like well-aged tawny ports, with their light, balanced sweetness and nutty mellowness. Take the Taylor Fladgate twenty-year-old tawny; lightly aromatic, with dark fig notes, it's rich on the palate but not thick or overtly sweet.

Moving into spirits, we've got to begin with cognac, the original sipping spirit. For nightcap use, you'll need to trade up to an XO grade; anything less is likely to be far too young and lively. Once you do shell out, though, a cognac such as the Delamain Pale & Dry XO makes the rewards obvious. It's as smooth and even delicate as you could hope for, but with a finish that keeps changing in your mouth, evolving; now juicy grapes, now baked apples, now nutmeg, cloves, cinnamon—if you didn't have to brush your teeth, you'd be tasting it all night.

A little bit beefier is the Powers John's Lane twelve-year-old pure pot still Irish whiskey. For those who know Powers as a bar whiskey, this is the same stuff grown older, richer, and stronger. (It's a respectable 92 proof.) It's got the same light-musky graininess, but it's thicker, even oilier on the tongue. When you're drinking it at the end of the night, you'll want to add a little splash of water—nothing more than a teaspoon or two—to calm it down.

Finally, there's the Plantation Vintage 2000 Trinidad rum. While the other three are all subtlety and elegance, this one's more bewitchment and intensity, a dark whirlpool of tar and burnt sugar and roasted tropical fruit that would be too much if it weren't so smooth. While the others persuade you to sleep, this one lures you into it.

Bar Rules

RULE NO. 30

Beer is food. Wine accompanies food. Cocktails demand food.

RULE NO. 43

The best song to drink to is still David Allan Coe's "You Never Even Called Me by My Name."

RULE NO. 90

No bar game requires warm-up stretching, crouching to examine the slope of a green, or calling for silence.

RULE NO. 92

Avoid bars that employ cute labels for the men's and women's rooms. If you can't, just remember: You're a pointer, not a setter; a buoy, not a gull; an XY, not an XX; a ▼, not a ▲.

RULE NO. 390

No matter your age, you're officially too old to order any drink that requires licking salt off another human being.

RULE NO. 692

If the bar's name ends in z, any relationship initiated there will not last. Including the relationship with the bar.

RULE NO. 699

Go ahead and order the pitcher.

Stinger

This simple mix of old cognac and white crème de menthe has been closing evenings since 1890 or thereabouts.

In a cocktail shaker, combine **2¼ oz [68 ml] XO-grade cognac** such as Martell Cordon Bleu, **¾ oz [22 ml] imported white crème de menthe**, and plenty of **ice** and shake hard. Strain into a chilled cocktail glass. **MAKES 1 DRINK**

BATCH DRINKS & PUNCHES

Because You Have Friends

BATCH DRINKS

~~~~~~

When you invite friends to your house for dinner, you don't show them where you keep the groceries and the kitchenware and let them feed themselves as best they can. And yet when they come over for cocktails, it's perfectly acceptable to steer them to a table with a bucket of ice; a random assortment of liquors; and some bottles of tonic, seltzer, and whatnot; and leave them to fend for themselves. Not very hospitable, when you think about it. Unless your friends are all bartenders, they end up stuck with booze on the rocks or, at best, two-ingredient highballs (okay, three if you count the lime wedge). Festive.

The solution, of course, is to serve your guests drinks. But just as you don't go around polling them about what they're in the mood to eat and then cook it all to order, you don't have to set up a full bar and play bartender all night, fielding orders for Long Island iced teas, Redheaded Sluts, and all the other mixological detritus that gets stuck in people's brains. There's a happy medium between benign neglect and masochism, and that medium is the cocktail list. Simply choose two to four cocktails, preferably elegant ones, print up a card with what you're offering, and, most important, batch them all up in advance. That way you won't have to fumble with jiggers and bottles and such. All you have to do come party time is shake and strain—the fun part.

Gin Daisy

A crisp and delightful classic, suitable for gin drinkers and gin haters alike.

In a large pitcher or mixing bowl, combine **one 750-ml bottle gin, 8 oz [240 ml] freshly squeezed and strained lemon juice, 4 oz [120 ml] Grand Marnier, 4 oz [120 ml] simple syrup** (see Sweetening, page 21), and lots of **ice** and stir well. Strain into glasses (about 2½ oz [80 ml] per serving) and top off with **a splash of chilled club soda** or seltzer water. Float **a fresh mint leaf** on top of each. **MAKES ABOUT 12 DRINKS**

Manhattan Club Manhattan

As served at the drink's birthplace, back in the 1880s.

In a large pitcher or mixing bowl, combine **one 750-ml bottle rye whiskey, one 750-ml bottle sweet vermouth, ½ oz [15 ml] orange bitters** or ¼ oz [10 ml] Angostura bitters, and lots of **ice** and stir well. Strain into glasses (about 3 oz [90 ml] per serving), twist **a swatch of thin-cut lemon peel** over the surface of each and drop it in. **MAKES ABOUT 16 DRINKS**

Michelada

If your idea of barbecuing involves marinating a big hunk of pork shoulder in garlic and lime juice, slow-cooking it until it practically melts, hacking it up, and serving it on corn tortillas with chopped onions and cilantro, then you're going to want to wash things down with something a lot tastier than light beer.

Put a **5-L Heineken draught keg** on ice. Squeeze the juice of **12 limes** into a pitcher. Add **¾ oz [22 ml] Worcestershire sauce**, **¾ oz [22 ml] Maggi seasoning** (a soy sauce–like product found online and in Mexican grocery shops), **¾ oz [22 ml] Mexican hot sauce** (Cholula works well), and (optionally) **4 oz [120 ml] good, smoky mezcal** and stir well. Refrigerate until well chilled. Fill tall (12-oz [360-ml]) glasses with **crushed ice.** If you wish, rub the outside rim of each glass with **a lime wedge** and roll the rims in **salt** to coat. Spoon a generous 1 Tbsp of the chilled spicy lime-juice mixture into each glass and top off with beer from the keg. **MAKES ABOUT 20 DRINKS**

Saint Valentine

An *Esquire* original. One of the crowd-pleasingest tipples we've ever made.

In a large pitcher or mixing bowl, combine **one 750-ml bottle full-flavored white rum** such as Havana Club three-year-old, Banks 5 Island, or Denizen; **8 oz [240 ml] Grand Marnier; 8 oz [240 ml] ruby port; 8 oz [240 ml] freshly squeezed and strained lime juice**; and lots of **ice** and stir well. Strain into glasses (about 3 oz [90 ml] per serving). **MAKES ABOUT 16 DRINKS**

Whiskey Lemonade

The only thing as refreshing as the Michelada (facing page) is this soothingly named lemonade, whose moniker is an underhanded way of getting everybody drinking a rollicking Irish whiskey punch. We make this in the summer; it's easy enough, although not too easy (everything good is worth working a little bit for), and delicious.

Juice **12 lemons**. Strain the juice and set aside. In a saucepan over low heat, dissolve **2 ¼ cups [450 g] Demerara sugar** in **2 cups [480 ml] water**, stirring until the sugar is dissolved. (If you've got raspberry bushes and ripe berries, you can mash **1 to 2 cups [120 to 240 g] ripe berries** into the hot syrup, strain out the seeds, and proceed as directed.) Remove the syrup from the heat and let cool. Stir in the lemon juice, then transfer the lemonade to a large (1-gl [3.8-L]) pitcher or jug. Add **2 qt [2 L] water** and **4 ½ cups [1 L] Irish whiskey** and stir well. Refrigerate until well chilled.
MAKES ABOUT 30 DRINKS

In Praise
of the

5-GALLON
IGLOO COOLER

BY DAVID WONDRICH

Managing a backyard full of tipsy friends is one of the great under-appreciated adult skills. It's easy to get people stinking drunk, if they're the drinking kind. Three rounds of real margaritas—the kind that's just good tequila, fresh lime juice, and Cointreau—before the food comes out and you might as well be entertaining so many ring-tailed lemurs for all the sense you'll get out of your guests. It's also easy to under-ethanolize them—just make free, but not too free, with the Pinot Grigio or light beer and watch the awkward pauses and covert glances at timepieces multiply.

For getting it just right, we know of nothing more effective than the 5-gallon Igloo cooler full of old-school punch. The vessel might not be elegant, but it keeps the cold in and the flies out, and after a couple cups of this punch—which bears as much resemblance to the swill usually dished out under its name as the gin martini does to the chocotini—nobody will give a damn what it's being served from. Not too strong, not too sweet, plenty refreshing, and tasting just boozy enough to remind you to go easy, it has the additional advantage of slowly getting weaker as the ice melts—in case you forget the go-easy part.

Charles Dickens's

PUNCH RITUAL

Here's how Dickens made punch for his friends. Best to do as he did and talk your way through everything as you go.

STEP 1

About three hours before your party, peel 3 lemons with a swivel-bladed vegetable peeler, trying to make one long spiral of peel from each. Put the lemon peels in a 3- or 4-qt [2.8- or 3.8-L] flame-proof bowl with ¾ cup [150 g] Demerara sugar or other raw sugar. Muddle the peels and sugar together and let sit.

STEP 2

Also before your party, squeeze enough lemons to make ¾ cup [180 ml] strained juice. Put the juice in a cup and refrigerate it. Pour 1 cup [240 ml] VSOP-grade cognac into a measuring pitcher or glass and set aside. In another pitcher or a bowl, combine 1¼ cups [300 ml] mellow amber rum, such as Mount Gay Eclipse or Angostura 1919, and 1¼ cups [300 ml] funky, strong (more than 55 percent alcohol) Jamaican rum, such as Smith & Cross.

STEP 3

Once your guests have arrived, in a saucepan over high heat, bring 1 qt [960 ml] water to boil. Put the bowl containing the lemon peels and sugar on a wooden cutting board or other heat-resistant surface in a spot where everyone can watch you work. When the water boils, remove from the heat. Gather your guests around the bowl and pour in the cognac and rum, noting what you're adding and why. Talking point: The lemon peels give rich lemony flavor, the cognac body, the rum bouquet— and flammability.

STEP 4

With a long-handled bar-spoon, remove a spoonful of the rum-cognac mix-ture. Holding it away from you and using a match or lighter, set on fire. Return the flaming spoon to the bowl, using it to ignite the rest. Stir with a ladle or long-handled spoon, attempting to dissolve the sugar. Let burn for 2 to 3 minutes, occasionally lifting one of the lemon peels up so people can admire the flames running down it. Talking point: You're setting the punch alight not because it looks cool but to burn off some of the more volatile elements of the alcohol. That's the story, anyway.

STEP 5

Extinguish the flames by covering the bowl with a tray and then stir in the reserved lemon juice and the hot water.

STEP 6

Grate fresh nutmeg over the top and ladle out in 3-oz [90-ml] servings.
MAKES 12 TO 16 DRINKS

Barbados Punch

On a hot day, there's nothing more refreshing or easier than putting out a bottle of mellow old rum, a bowl of ice, and a pitcher of cold coconut water. But that's not the only way to dispense those ingredients.

In a 3-qt [2.8-L] bowl, combine **¾ cup [150 g] superfine sugar** and **6 oz [180 ml] freshly squeezed lime juice** and stir until the sugar is dissolved. Fill the bowl three-fourths full of **ice cubes**. Add **one 750-ml bottle Bols Genever rum** or Mount Gay Eclipse rum, **2 cups [480 ml] coconut water**, and **2 cups [480 ml] water**. Stir. Ladle into glasses. Drink. **MAKES ABOUT 10 DRINKS**

The Bishop

Here's a drink that's as delightful as it is historic. (Dickens drank bowls of it. And he drank it warm.) For a little more bite, add 4 oz [120 ml] cognac along with the port.

Wash **an orange**, stud it with **16 to 18 cloves**, put it in a baking dish, and roast in a 350°F [180°C] oven until the skin is nicely browned in spots, 60 to 90 minutes. Remove from the oven and set aside to cool. In a saucepan over medium-high heat, combine **one 750-ml bottle ruby port** and **1 cup [240 ml] water** and bring to a simmer. Add **⅓ cup [65 g] sugar** and **a pinch each peeled and grated fresh ginger, freshly grated nutmeg, and ground allspice.** Cut the roasted orange into quarters. Add it to the port mixture along with any juices that run out and stir well. Serve in small glasses. **MAKES ABOUT 10 DRINKS**

Hot Punches →

When days are short and we're all huddling together for warmth, a largish quantity of something festive to drink is a deeply appreciated thing. So appreciated that the person who supplies it might become exempt from supplying anything else. What we're trying to say is: Punch is a gift.

Claret Cup

A good Claret Cup will perk up an afternoon affair without causing unseemly revelry.

In a large bowl, combine **one 750-ml bottle red Bordeaux, 4 oz [120 ml] amontillado sherry, 2 oz [60 ml] maraschino liqueur, the thin-cut peel of 1 whole lemon**, and **¼ cup [50 g] superfine sugar** and just "let stand an hour or so for interjubilation of ingredients," as our Lawton Mackall advised the prospective cup-brewer back in 1939. Then, add as big a berg of ice as you can produce (see Preparing Ice, page 19), gently stir in **4½ cups [1 L] chilled club soda**, and deck out with **a few sprigs of fresh mint**, if desired. (A curl of fresh cucumber rind would not go amiss, either.) **MAKES ABOUT 20 DRINKS**

The Fatal Bowl

True punch is as complex and darkly invigorating as a Manhattan and as quaffable as a good Pinot Noir, while being more alcoholic than both. Oh, and if you make it with tea, as the gents used to, it's got a nice, cracky edge to it.

The day before your punch party, place a 2-qt [2-L] bowl of water in the freezer to make an ice block. Also that day, using a swivel-bladed vegetable peeler, remove the colorful peel from **6 lemons** and put the peels in a 1-qt [960-ml] mason jar. Add **1 cup [200 g] fine-grain raw sugar**, seal the jar, shake well, and let stand overnight. This will infuse the sugar with lemon oil.

The day of the party, unseal the jar, add **1 cup [240 ml] freshly squeezed and strained lemon juice**, reseal the jar, and shake until the sugar is dissolved; this is your "shrub," or traditional punch base. Meanwhile, bring **1 qt [960 ml] water** to a boil, remove from the heat, and add **4 tea bags** (English Breakfast works well). After 5 minutes, remove the tea bags and let the tea cool.

Pour the shrub into a 1-gl [3.8-L] bowl, peels and all. Add the brewed tea, **2½ cups [600 ml] VSOP-grade cognac** or Armagnac, and **1½ cups [360 ml] dark, full-bodied and funky rum** such as Smith & Cross. Stir well and let cool in the refrigerator for an hour or so. To serve, slip your block of ice into the punch bowl, grate **fresh nutmeg** over the top, and dish the nectar forth with your silver punch ladle (you've got one of those, right?). **MAKES ABOUT 30 DRINKS**

Spread Eagle Punch

This American classic (the recipe is from Jerry Thomas's 1862 *How to Mix Drinks*, the world's first bartenders' guide) is a foil for the fruity slop that so often passes for holiday punch. Dry, rich, and both smoky and lemony, it leverages the healing power of whiskey to create something that's masculine enough for your uncle but not so intense that your coworkers won't lap it up.

Forty-eight hours before your party, put a 1-gl [3.8-L] bowl of water in the freezer to make an ice block. The day before, prepare a double batch of oleo-saccharum (see Oleo-saccharum, page 22), using a 1-qt [960-ml] mason jar, **1½ cups [300 g] sugar**, and the **peels of 8 lemons**. The day of the party, add **1½ cups [360 ml] freshly squeezed and strained lemon juice** to the jar, reseal, and shake until sugar is dissolved. Pour the contents of the jar into a 5-gl [19-L] bowl and add **two 750-ml bottles smoky single-malt Scotch** (Bowmore Legend is good and affordable, but Laphroaig will work well, too) and **two 750-ml bottles straight rye whiskey** (Sazerac rye is particularly fine here). Stir well, then add **1 gl [3.8 L] water.**

　　To serve, unmold your ice block and carefully slide it into the bowl. Add **4 thinly sliced and seeded lemons** and grate **fresh nutmeg** over the top.
MAKES ABOUT 48 DRINKS

A LITTLE SOMETHING
TO EAT, MAYBE?

Delicious Snacks from a Few of Esquire's Favorite Chefs

Potato Chips with Crème Fraîche and Caviar

BRYCE SHUMAN, Betony, New York City

Caviar can seem so posh, but potato chips keep it cool and casual. The crunchy chips are the perfect contrast to the silky crème fraîche and little pops of nutty sturgeon roe. This high-low artful appetizer is fun for a party—or a late afternoon snack on the porch with a clean, simple drink.

---

8 oz [230 g] crème fraîche
Pinch of salt
Lime wedge
1 Tbsp minced fresh chives
1 large bag good-quality potato chips
One 2- to 4-oz [55- to 115-g] jar sturgeon or trout roe, such as Petrossian Tsar Imperial caviar

In a small bowl, combine the crème fraîche, salt, and a few drops of lime juice. Whisk until light and airy. Scoop into a serving bowl and garnish with the chives. Serve with the potato chips and caviar. Dip chips into the crème fraîche and spoon on as much or as little caviar as you like. **SERVES 4**

Almonds with Sea Salt and Rosemary

DONALD LINK, Herbsaint, New Orleans

Of course everyone relates the idea of salty snacks—pretzels, bar peanuts—with beer drinking, but this version of roasted almonds is a little more refined, using great olive oil, sea salt, and just a touch of rosemary to complement a cocktail's nuanced flavors.

---

1 lb [455 g] raw, unsalted
  almonds
2 tsp extra-virgin olive oil
  (the good kind)
Fleur de sel sea salt
¼ tsp chopped fresh
  rosemary
¼ tsp cayenne pepper, or
  to taste
1 Tbsp sherry or balsamic
  vinegar (optional)

Preheat the oven to 300°F [150°C].

Spread the almonds on a baking sheet and roast until fragrant, 5 to 10 minutes, stirring once about halfway through.

While still hot, pour the almonds into a bowl and toss with the olive oil, 2 tsp salt, rosemary, cayenne, and vinegar (if using). Taste for salt and add more, if you like. Same goes for the cayenne. **SERVES 8**

Deviled Eggs with Pickles and Bacon

LINTON HOPKINS, Restaurant Eugene, Atlanta

A deviled egg's creamy, rich texture acts as a counterpoint to a cocktail's sharp alcohol bite. The smoked paprika and black pepper also add interest. These are excellent with whiskey cocktails, which have a rustic, sweet smokiness that plays off the deviled eggs' natural characteristics, and with Champagne cocktails—the effervescence cuts through the richness.

6 eggs
1 tsp yellow mustard, such as French's or Plochman's
2 or 3 dashes Tabasco sauce
½ Tbsp grated onion
3 Tbsp mayonnaise
¼ tsp coarsely ground black pepper
Kosher salt
Smoked hot paprika for dusting
1 tsp minced fresh parsley
1 tsp crisp-cooked crumbled bacon
1 tsp minced bread-and-butter pickles

Place the eggs in a saucepan and cover with cold water. Bring to a boil, stirring gently in the beginning to set the yolks in the middles. Once the water is boiling, cook for 10 minutes, then immediately transfer the eggs to ice water. When cool, peel the eggs and cut in half lengthwise. Remove the yolks and put them in a bowl. Set the whites aside. Mash the yolks with a fork, then add the mustard, Tabasco, onion, mayonnaise, black pepper, and ¼ tsp salt and mix well. Season the egg whites with salt and spoon the yolk mixture into each cavity. Dust with paprika, then garnish with the parsley, bacon, and pickles before serving. **SERVES 6**

Bacon-Wrapped Jalapeños Stuffed with Pineapple and Kielbasa

JOSIAH CITRIN, Mélisse, Los Angeles

These jalapeños are smoky, salty, sweet, and hot, and they can really punch through a drink that has a high alcohol content. Mezcal and tequila play especially well with the smokiness of the bacon. Note: If scaling up for a crowd, try grilling the assembled jalapeños. Build a hot fire in a charcoal grill and let it burn down to medium heat, or preheat a gas grill to medium. Arrange the jalapeños on the grill rack and cook, turning often, until heated through and the bacon is crisp on all sides, about 20 minutes.

1 kielbasa
2 ripe pineapple spears
6 large jalapeño chiles, stemmed, seeds scooped out, chiles kept whole
6 large fresh basil leaves
6 strips bacon

Preheat the oven to 450°F [230°C].

Fill a saucepan with water and heat until simmering. Add the kielbasa and poach for 20 minutes.

Cut the pineapple spears into six pieces, each about ½ in [12 mm] wide and 1½ in [4 cm] long. When the kielbasa is ready, cut it into six pieces about the size of your thumb or smaller, depending on what you can fit inside the jalapeños.

Stuff each jalapeño with a piece of pineapple and a piece of kielbasa and wrap with a basil leaf, then wrap again with a piece of bacon. Skewer the jalapeños with a sturdy toothpick to hold the wrapping in place.

Arrange the skewered chiles in a cast-iron skillet and fry over medium heat until the bacon is golden on all sides, turning as needed. Transfer the skillet to the oven and roast to cook through and finish crisping the bacon, about 15 minutes. Serve hot. **SERVES 8**

Shiitake Mushroom Yakitori

TAKASHI YAGIHASHI, Takashi, Chicago

Yakitori—small, charcoal-grilled skewers of meat or vegetables—is Japanese comfort food and a staple at *izakayas* (informal drinking establishments). These mushrooms, marinated in ginger, soy, and red pepper flakes, are both earthy and piquant, and contrast nicely with simple, refreshing cocktails. The Tukedare Sauce can be made up to a week in advance; store in a tightly sealed container in the refrigerator.

TUKEDARE SAUCE

1 cup [240 ml] Japanese
  soy sauce
¾ cup [340 g] honey
1 ½ Tbsp sake
1 ½ Tbsp water
1 Tbsp sesame oil
1 ½ tsp peeled and grated
  fresh ginger (optional)
½ tsp red pepper flakes

30 shiitake mushrooms,
  stemmed and brushed
  clean

Build a hot fire in a charcoal grill and let burn down to medium heat, about 20 minutes; preheat a gas grill to medium; or heat a grill pan over medium heat.

To make the Tukedare Sauce: In a bowl, whisk together the soy sauce, honey, sake, water, sesame oil, ginger (if using), and red pepper flakes.

Add the mushrooms to the sauce, toss to coat, and let marinate for 15 minutes. Thread four or five mushrooms on six 6-in [15-cm] wooden skewers. Spear the mushroom caps on the diagonal so they will lie flat on the grill or pan. Leave room at the ends as handles so the skewers are easy to turn. Arrange the skewers on the grill rack or in the pan and grill, turning every 2 minutes or so, until the mushrooms are slightly charred all over and softened, about 6 minutes total. Serve warm or at room temperature. **SERVES 6**

Smoked Bluefish Rillettes

BARBARA LYNCH, Drink, Boston

Smoked fish pairs well with lighter cocktails, like serving oysters with Champagne. Here, the smoking process mitigates the fishiness we tend to associate with bluefish and curing imparts a pleasant saltiness that reveals rich and creamy layers. It's the perfect foil for sherry-based cocktails, or the notes of caraway or juniper in gin, which bring out the fish's oceanic flavors. Make the pickled onions the day before, or skip those and substitute thinly sliced shallots.

PICKLED RED ONIONS

1 ½ cups [360 ml] distilled
   white vinegar
½ cup [100 g] sugar
⅓ cup [65 g] kosher salt
1 Tbsp black peppercorns
1 red onion

RILLETTES

6 oz [170 g] smoked bluefish,
   mackerel, or trout, flaked
2 Tbsp crème fraîche
2 Tbsp freshly squeezed
   lemon juice
1 Tbsp minced fresh chives
Freshly ground black pepper
Kosher salt

12 slices sourdough bread
2 Tbsp olive oil
Leaves from 4 sprigs fresh
   flat-leaf parsley
Leaves from 4 stalks celery
2 lemons, cut into wedges

To make the pickled onions: In a small saucepan, combine the vinegar, sugar, salt, and peppercorns and bring to a boil over medium heat, stirring to help dissolve the salt and sugar. Meanwhile, thinly slice the onion and place in a heatproof glass container with a tight-fitting lid. Once the pickling liquid has come to a boil, carefully pour it over the onion, cover, and refrigerate overnight.

To make the rillettes: In a bowl, combine the bluefish, crème fraîche, lemon juice, chives, and ½ tsp pepper and stir to combine. Season with salt.

Build a hot fire in a charcoal grill or preheat a gas grill to high. Arrange the bread slices on the grill rack and grill, turning once, until well toasted, about 2 minutes per side. Drizzle each slice with ½ tsp olive oil.

Taste and adjust the seasoning of the rillettes with salt and pepper. Transfer to a serving bowl and garnish with the parsley and celery leaves. Serve with the grilled bread, pickled onions, and lemon wedges. **SERVES 6**

Index